A BRIEF HISTORY OF THE PRESBYTERIANS

A Brief History of the

PRESBYTERIANS

Revised and Enlarged

By LEFFERTS A. LOETSCHER

Professor of American Church History
Princeton Theological Seminary
Princeton, New Jersey

THE WESTMINSTER PRESS

Philadelphia

PRINTED IN THE UNITED STATES OF AMERICA

To my Mother
Mary McClelland Loetscher

CONTENTS

PAGE

Preface 9

I From the Apostles to the Reformers................. 11

II Two Great Reformers............................. 20

III The Presbyterians on the Continent of Europe......... 27

IV The Presbyterians in Scotland and Ireland............ 33

V The Presbyterians in England, Wales,
   and the British Dominions......................... 41

VI The Presbytery 49

VII The General Synod.............................. 55

VIII The General Assembly Organized 62

IX The Plan of Union.............................. 69

X The Church Divided............................. 76

XI The Church Reunited............................ 85

XII Recent Trends 94

XIII The United Presbyterian Church of North America..... 103

XIV Conclusion 110

Questions for Thought and Discussion............... 117

Bibliography 123

PREFACE TO THE REVISED AND ENLARGED EDITION

A BRIEF HISTORY OF THE PRESBYTERIANS *was originally written in connection with the celebration of the Sesquicentennial of the General Assembly in 1938. It was prepared as an "elective" course for young people in the church school curriculum, but enjoyed a wider usefulness in young people's societies, communicants classes, and adult groups, as well as among other laymen and ministers.*

When, after fifteen printings, the plates recently became worn out, it was necessary to reset type. This has given the opportunity to revise the text extensively where this seemed desirable in the light of recent scholarship or for other reasons, and to add new material covering the eventful two decades since original publication.

Brief questions for discussion groups or individual readers are provided near the end of the booklet, and the bibliography has been revised to include titles on the history of American Presbyterianism that have appeared in recent years.

New material deals with currents of religious thought and methods of church work stimulated by the social and cultural upheaval following upon two world wars, and comes to a kind of climax in the union of the Presbyterian Church in the U.S.A. and the United Presbyterian Church in North America to form the United Presbyterian Church in the U.S.A. One of the new chapters is devoted to sketching the history of the United Presbyterian Church in North America. It is hoped that one service of this revised booklet may be a modest contribution toward helping former "U.S.A." Presbyterians and former "U.P." Presbyterians to get better acquainted by appreciating more fully the great and somewhat different heritage which each brings to the common service of the Master.

CHAPTER I

From the Apostles to the Reformers

Presbyterianism. The New Testament, in telling of the beginnings of the Christian church, does not describe in detail any particular form of church government. Such intimations as are given, however, indicate that the primitive local congregations were led locally by ordained men known as "presbyters" or "elders." The name "Presbyterian" comes from the Greek word for "presbyter," and the Presbyterian Church believes that its form of government is in harmony with that set forth in The Acts of the Apostles and in the Epistles.

Scholarly studies of the primitive church have made it clear that the exact type of government then in use varied from place to place, and that it is impossible to claim that any present-day form of church government was divinely ordained in the days of the apostles for all time and has been divinely perpetuated to the present day. With the passage of time church government, reflecting the temper of the times, became increasingly autocratic. As a consequence, such representative government of a Presbyterian type as existed in the early church gradually receded into the background and was not restored on any large scale until the time of the Protestant Reformation in the sixteenth century, when it was extensively revived by the Reformed churches, of which John Calvin was the most conspicuous leader.

It will be the task of the present chapter to sketch very briefly the story of the fifteen centuries of Christianity from the time of the apostles to the time of the emergence of the Presbyterian type of church government under the Protestant reformers of the sixteenth century.

A Christian Church in a Heathen World. "Make disciples of all the nations," Jesus Christ commanded his followers (Matt. 28: 19). The missionary success of the earliest disciples is familiar to every reader of the New Testament, the apostle Paul himself traveling up and down the Empire, winning converts in Syria, Asia Minor, Greece, and Italy. After the death of the apostles, Christianity continued to spread with amazing speed, especially among the slaves and lower classes.

In the Roman Empire the prevailing heathenism was closely associated with the political government. When, therefore, the Christians refused to worship any deity except the one God, they were intermittently persecuted for almost three hundred years as traitors and "atheists." There is no nobler story in Christian annals than that of these unnamed heroes—many of them women and children—who chose death in the flames or at the jaws of wild beasts in the arena rather than renounce their divine Master. Polycarp, bishop of Smyrna, when commanded to repudiate Christ, replied with fearless dignity: "Fourscore and six years have I been serving him, and he hath done me no wrong. How then can I blaspheme my King who has saved me?" These faithful witnesses did not die in vain, for the blood of the martyrs became the seed of the church, and converts joined the courageous survivors in increasing numbers.

Christianity on the Throne of the Caesars. To Constantine the Great goes the credit for permanently changing the official status of the persecuted Christians. Legend tells us that Constantine, shortly before battle with a rival claimant for the throne, saw in clear daylight a shining cross in the sky with the words on it, "By this conquer." It is a known fact that, immediately following this experience, he had the shields of his soldiers inscribed with the sign of the cross, and crushed his rival in battle.

A Christian, in profession at least, was now on the throne of the Caesars. The benefits to the church were immediate. Christian laymen and bishops, instead of being persecuted, were advanced to positions of honor in the government. Church property was thereafter ordinarily exempted from taxation. Legislation now reflected something of the spirit of Christianity. Combats to the death between gladiators were on the way to being abolished. Marriage laws were improved. The lot of the slave was bettered. Sabbath laws were enacted. The church, with its increased prestige and wealth, was enabled to enrich its worship with the embellishments of architecture, sculpture, painting, and other arts. Christianity had become the government's pet child.

But the church's new and unaccustomed position of privilege was not an unmixed blessing. Christianity was no longer something to suffer for, but something to profit by. Following the example of their emperor, unconverted heathen flocked to the church, bringing in with them many of their heathen immoralities and religious beliefs. Even the clergy became secularized and worldly. Church affairs were now hopelessly entangled with court politics. Christian leaders, from their new vantage point, could use the government's authority to persecute heretics. Some of the more spiritual churchmen looked away wistfully from the newly acquired wealth and honor to the day, now past, when to be a Christian had sometimes involved making the supreme sacrifice of life itself.

Theology. From the beginning, Christians have heeded the command, "Thou shalt love the Lord thy God . . . with all thy mind" (Luke 10: 27). "Theology" is the effort to think as honestly and clearly as possible about Christian faith.

In the earliest years of the church Christian teachers were satisfied merely to repeat the language of the New Testament and Old Testament writings. But soon the deeper implications of these simple Scriptural statements were explored. Men asked, for example, exactly what we mean when we say that the Savior is the Son of God. Partly in order to settle, if possible, a controversy which had arisen around this particular problem, Christian bishops from all parts of the Empire met in council at Nicaea, a little town near modern Constantinople, in A.D. 325. The emperor Constantine convened the meeting and himself presided. This council came to the conclusion that the Son of God was never created, but has always existed, and is of the same divine spiritual "substance" as God the Father himself. Another council, in the next century, declared that Christ has two distinct natures, human and divine, united in a single person. Thus the church endeavored, according to the best terminology available in that day, to assert the absolute deity of the Savior. This continues to be the official belief of all of the major Christian bodies throughout the world.

These doctrines concerned the nature of the Trinity and the Person of Christ. About this time, Augustine, a keen-minded and hot-blooded man living on the southern shores of the Mediterranean, had a profound experience of deliverance, by the grace of God, from shameful immoralities and from years of painful groping after religious truth. His experiences and convictions, as set down in his *Confessions* and other works, were the foundation on which the church later built many of its doctrines of human sin and the absolute need of the human soul for the help of God's Spirit.

Rome Falls. To the north of the Roman Empire, while these theological discussions were in progress, roamed hardy Germanic tribes, disdainfully called "barbarians" by the highly civilized Romans. For centuries the Roman legions on the Rhine and the Danube had repelled their assaults, but in the year 410, less than a century after Constantine's conversion, Alaric, a barbarian chieftain, captured the "eternal city" of Rome itself. Before long other barbarian hordes swept in, and occupied all the western part of the former Roman Empire. A new epoch in human history, the so-called "Middle Ages," was beginning.

The immediate damage done to the Christian church and to society was incalculable. Countless buildings, art treasures, literary works, and the accumulated wealth of centuries were swept away with a stroke. Many centers of civilization were reduced to the level of semi-barbarism for centuries to come.

Above the floods of barbarism and conquest the church stood like "a city set on a hill." In its monasteries and vaults were preserved precious copies of the Scriptures, as well as the writings of the Christian teachers, or "church fathers," and the classical literature of antiquity. Amidst the prevailing brutality and lawlessness, the church never entirely forgot its gospel of divine love and self-sacrificing service. The Christian church was to prove itself the light of the "Dark Ages."

Foreign Missions. In the history of Christianity there have been three great missionary, or expansive, epochs, the first two of which lie within the period covered by the present chapter: (1) The evangelization of the Roman Empire by the original apostles and their successors during the first three centuries. (2) The Christianization of the barbarians from the fifth to the eleventh centuries. (3) The modern Protestant missionary movement, simultaneous with the commercial penetration of non-Christian lands.

The second period, that of evangelizing the barbarian conquerors of the Empire, is inferior to neither of the other periods in its importance and dramatic interest. A monk who was soon to become Pope Gregory the Great, seeing three Anglo-Saxon boys from Britain for sale in the slave market at Rome, was impressed with their handsome blue eyes and fair complexions. He asked who they were, and was told that they were Angles. He answered, "Not Angles, but angels, for they have angelic faces, and are worthy to be fellow heirs with angels in heaven." Gregory sent Augustine (not the theologian) to them as missionary. The half-legendary Patrick labored as missionary in Ireland, Columba in Scotland, Boniface in Germany, Ansgar in Scandinavia, Cyril and Methodius among the Slavs.

It is as a result of the labors of these missionaries and others like them that the great nations of Europe and America today are Christian. If there be those who would disparage the foreign missionary movement of our own time, let them recall the lasting effect on world history of this early period of missions.

The Pope. In the earliest years of the Christian movement little attention seems to have been paid to the form of church government. Very soon, however, the clergy emerged as a distinct class. In order that the church organization might be strong to resist persecution, bishops gradually arose, who had authority over the lower clergy.

The bishop of Rome, the capital city of the Empire, gradually acquired unique prestige. When the barbarians invaded the Empire in the fifth century, and swept away the old governments, the Christian church seemed to be the only surviving bulwark. In such a crisis men desired a strong church with a strong head. The bishop of Rome was the natural man to fill the breach, and was now readily accorded the authority of pope, or "father," of the church. The papacy, in supplying vigorous, even if autocratic, leadership during these dark centuries performed an inestimable service to Christianity and to civilization.

As time passed, the popes claimed increasing authority. Pope Gregory VII, in the eleventh century, claimed to be the representative of God on earth, and declared that kings and emperors held their power only during his good pleasure. Gregory was powerful enough to force the German emperor to do penance before him in the snow for three days. The papacy reached its greatest power under Pope Innocent III, in the early thirteenth century. Perhaps no king or emperor in history has ever before or since wielded the power that this man held. Kings and emperors did his bidding. No man dared to contradict him. His rule marked the high point of papal power. After his time national patriotism began to awaken in Europe, and nations refused to be ruled from Rome. But the papacy never retracted its claims to world dominion.

Monasteries. Back in the days of the emperor Constantine, a man named Anthony withdrew into the deserts of Egypt, where he lived on bread, water, and dates, wore a hair shirt and a sheepskin, and slept on the bare ground. He spent most of his days and nights in prayer. In view of the corruption that Constantine's conversion was bringing into the church, countless Christians, instead of endeavoring to purify the church, withdrew to pious solitude, following the example of Anthony.

The pious recluses soon organized into groups, or monasteries. In their misguided zeal they renounced personal possessions and marriage. In the centuries of banditry and ignorance that immediately followed the barbarian invasions, the monasteries were a light in the darkness. Monks preserved the ancient learning by copying priceless manuscripts by hand, and, in a world run wild with bloodshed and lawlessness, kept alive Christian faith and the Christian ideal of self-renunciation.

Though the monasteries produced some of the finest of the popes, and noble spirits like Bernard of Clairvaux, whose hymns we still sing, the monasteries themselves in time became appallingly corrupt. The oathbound renunciation of marriage produced abominable evils.

Though the monks individually were poor, the monastic institutions themselves were often wealthy, supporting the inmates in idleness and self-indulgence. Before the end of the Middle Ages, the monasteries, originally founded in the spirit of earnest piety, had become a public scandal. Their history shows conclusively that the Christian's life should be in the world, though not of it.

Christian Worship. The earliest worship of the Christians seems to have been very simple. Justin Martyr, in the second century, tells us that they met on Sunday, heard a reading from the Old Testament or a Gospel, followed by a sermon. Then they rose for prayer, after which the Communion was celebrated. Hymns were sung to Christ as to God.

With the passing of time simple things become more complex. So it was with Christian worship. After the era of persecution ended, a halo gathered around the heads of the Christian martyrs. Their very bones—called "relics"—were said to possess miraculous healing powers. Their prayers were thought to be more efficacious than the prayers of living Christians. Mary, the mother of Jesus, was honored as the chief of these "saints." Then, too, Christians sought to make their faith more vivid by the use of pictures and images of Christ and of the saints. They even addressed prayers to Mary and the saints, frequently while facing holy pictures and images, until some critics began to wonder whether Christianity was not sinking to the level of the heathen idolatry which it had displaced. In the celebration of the Communion the idea gradually arose that God, at a certain moment, miraculously transformed the bread and wine into the actual body and blood of Christ, though these still retained the outward appearance and taste of mere bread and wine. Unscrupulous priests sometimes used this belief as a means of demanding exorbitant fees for themselves. In the later centuries of the Middle Ages, great cathedrals, usually with their ground plan in the form of a cross, rose all over Europe. Many of these still stand as noble monuments to medieval piety.

The Crusades. The Crusades were a strange, bloody interpretation of Christianity. When, in the eleventh century, the Turks conquered the Holy Land and insulted and enslaved the Christian pilgrims who were journeying there, the pope, powerfully supported by a strange popular orator named Peter the Hermit, urged that the Christians of Europe rescue the holy places. The First Crusade was the most successful, and captured Jerusalem within three years. The Third Crusade was the most colorful, being led by Frederick of Germany, Philip Augustus of France, and Richard I of England, the last named familiar to all readers of Scott's *Ivanhoe*. There were seven Crusades, and even a Children's Crusade, with children from France and Germany dying in the cold of the Alps, or lost at sea, or sold to slave dealers.

The Crusades were a pathetically misdirected form of Christian zeal, but they had indirectly a very stimulating effect on Europe. Men from different countries mingled in the crusaders' camps, and national patriotism was developed. The travel to distant parts of the world and contact with strange men and customs had their broadening effect on thousands. The last of the Crusades, in the thirteenth century, found Palestine once more in the hands of the Mohammedans, but it found Europe about to leave the medieval period of childhood and to enter into the maturity of modern times.

The Corruption of the Church. It is the noblest things that are capable of the deepest degradation. Both the Old Testament and the New Testament, with their Balaams and Caiaphases, warn that even the noblest offices, in unclean hands, can become utterly corrupt.

The Middle Ages—that period between the barbarian conquests and the Protestant Reformation—had innumerable noble Christian elements in it, as we have seen. But as the period drew toward a close it seemed as though the church's power to reform itself was exhausted. The monasteries, at first oases in the desert of barbarian invasion, had lost their spiritual vigor. The papacy, once a mighty force against lawlessness and anarchy, and at times even a power for reform, had itself become, for the moment, the center of corruption. Such a pope as Alexander VI, of the Borgia family, who was sunk in every kind of vice—covetousness, perfidy, adultery, murder—is not typical of the popes who either preceded him or followed him, but he is typical of his own day. Church worship, once a source of inspiration and strength to Christians, had now become, in large parts of the so-called "Christian" world, merely a thing of blind superstition and a means of wealth to the higher clergy. Conditions in the church cried aloud for reformation, and the living God was about to answer the need of his people.

CHAPTER II

Two Great Reformers

Martin Luther. God chose a miner's son, Martin Luther (1483-1546), to lead his church from corruption to a truer knowledge of the living God. In his sincere but misguided zeal, Martin Luther sought peace of soul by becoming a monk. Though he had always lived an upright life, and though in the monastery he devoted himself to religious ceremonies and activities, he could attain no assurance that God had forgiven his sins. A fellow monk reminded him of the phrase in the Apostles' Creed, "I believe in . . . the forgiveness of sins." Luther read in Paul's Epistle, "The righteous shall live by faith" (Rom. 1: 17). At last the great truth dawned on him: prolonged fasting, performance of mysterious ceremonies, payment of exorbitant fees to priests and churches, unnatural renunciation of life's wholesome things, cannot earn God's favor. To be pleasing to God, he saw, a man must trust in Jesus Christ with his whole mind and heart. This truth, so familiar to us of today, was soon to prove itself a world-shaking discovery.

About this time the pope, who was in need of funds to build St. Peter's Cathedral at Rome, arranged for a sale of "indulgences," by which the purchasers were supposed to be delivered from certain punishments after death. This was too much for Luther, with his newly found knowledge of the way to God by simple faith in Christ, and in the year 1517 he nailed to the door of the castle church at Wittenberg—which was often used as a kind of bulletin board—ninety-five "theses," or propositions, attacking the whole system of indulgences. To Luther's own amazement this simple act started the Protestant Reformation, for the response was nation-wide.

The pope could not allow such insubordination to pass undisciplined, and sent a "bull," or official order, excommunicating Luther. Luther replied by publicly burning the bull, an act symbolizing his rejection of papal authority. In view of the church's great political and financial power, this required tremendous courage. Would Luther's countrymen stand with him, or with the old church?

In 1521 the emperor who ruled Germany, Charles V, convened a "diet," or national parliament, at Worms amidst great pomp and splendor. Luther was brought before this diet and ordered to recant, or repudiate, the things he had written against the Roman Church. As he stood there before the princes and nobles of the Empire, this peasant's son gave the simple answer: "I shall not retract one iota, so Christ help me." Tradition says that he replied further: "Here I stand. I cannot do otherwise. God help me! Amen." Luther had fought and won his battle. He had openly defied a corrupt church and its princely supporters, and had come away without surrendering a single one of his principles.

On his way home, Luther was seized by armed horsemen and forcibly carried to the Wartburg Castle. Fortunately this was only an act of friends, to hide him from the possible vengeance of his enemies. While at the Wartburg, Luther translated the New Testament from the original Greek into German, and, a few years after leaving the castle, he translated the Old Testament from the original Hebrew. Laymen could now compare the new Protestant teachings with the Bible for themselves.

The old erroneous idea that only an unmarried person can achieve the highest degree of purity and holiness, and that therefore priests should never marry, had soiled the church with immoralities. Luther declared that a faithful married life is as pleasing to God as virginity, and proved his sincerity by marrying Catherine von Bora when he was forty-two years old. Here too history has proved the soundness of his teaching.

"Martin Luther . . . is one of the few men of whom it may be said that the history of the world was profoundly altered by his work." He broke the autocratic power of a then tyrannical church, and declared that Christianity is primarily personal trust in God as we know him in Jesus Christ. Virtue, he taught, consists in the use and consecration to God of the ordinary relationships and tasks of life, rather than in their renunciation.

Southern Germany remained Catholic, but Lutheranism soon became the dominant faith of northern Germany, as well as of the Scandinavian countries, Norway, Sweden, and Denmark.

John Calvin. Unfortunately Protestantism was soon divided into two great groups—Lutheran and Reformed. The Lutheran, as the name implies, was led by Martin Luther; the Reformed, or Presbyterian, by John Calvin. One regrets that differences of viewpoint on the Lord's Supper and certain other doctrines were permitted to divide the forces of Protestantism, a division that has continued to our own day.

John Calvin (1509-1564), a Frenchman born in Noyon, France, was the chief formulator of Presbyterianism. Protestants before him had suggested some of his ideas, and later followers made changes, but Calvin more than any other one man gave to Presbyterianism its distinctive character. He had originally expected to become a lawyer, and had studied in three leading French universities. When he was twenty-three or twenty-four he was suddenly converted to Protestant Christianity, though he tells us nothing of the details of the experience. Persecution that broke out soon afterward against Protestants in France caused him to flee to Switzerland and then to Italy.

In 1536, when still in his twenty-seventh year, Calvin published the first edition of his famous *Institutes of the Christian Religion*. It was the best statement of Protestant faith that had yet appeared, and at once marked the young author as a leader of the new movement. In the *Institutes* and in all of his writing, Calvin's main interest was in Jesus Christ as God come in human flesh. God's Truth, he believed, is not wordy speculation, but is Jesus Christ Himself. Calvin devoted a large part of his life to explaining the meaning of the Bible, which he tried to understand in relation to Christ. He did not treat the Bible in a mechanical way as a textbook of statements about God, but as a record of God's grace which the Holy Spirit repeatedly causes to "come alive" for the Christian reader.

Calvin's emphasis on God's grace led him to the doctrine of election—the belief that the Christian is able to choose God only because

God has first irresistibly chosen him. The idea, as Calvin held it, is deeply religious, but unprofitable speculations were sometimes drawn from it, especially after Calvin's time. He had much to say about God's sovereignty, that is, his rule over men and over all creation. Calvin had a high view of the organized or "visible" church as our necessary and beloved spiritual "mother." Throughout his life he opposed divisions in the church, and advocated and worked for Christian unity. His religious thought is many-sided, like the Bible after which he patterned it, containing even seeming contradictions held in balance. He was broader in outlook and sympathy than has sometimes been realized, and often deliberately chose a middle view between extremes.

In the same year in which he published his *Institutes,* Calvin was passing through Geneva, Switzerland, intending to spend a single night there. But Farel, a Protestant preacher of the place, told him that God was calling him to remain and labor in this city, and that if he preferred scholarly leisure to the clear voice of duty, the curse of God would rest upon him. Conscience-smitten, Calvin remained to labor in Geneva. Within two years, however, he and Farel were banished from the city for resisting efforts by the civil government to interfere in church matters. But affairs in Geneva suffered from the loss of Calvin's strong leadership, and, invited back, he returned after three years of exile.

Back once again in Geneva, Calvin developed one of his most distinctive achievements—Presbyterian church government. He provided for four types of church officers: pastors, teachers, elders, and deacons. The clergy were equal, without superior bishops over them, and the lay elders, twelve in number, were elected by the civil magistrates from their own number, to share with the clergy in church government. These principles paralleled the representative civil government that had emerged in such commercial cities as Geneva, and would contribute greatly in later years toward the further development of democracy in the Western world.

The ministers met by themselves every week for discussion and every quarter year for self-discipline. Church government for the whole city was exercised by one "consistory" composed of all the ministers and the twelve elders. This consistory performed the function of church discipline. Calvin thought of Christian living as free life in Christ. "We are not our own, but the Lord's," he said. But Christian freedom for him meant Christlike life as set forth in the Scriptures, not moral laxity. The Geneva consistory undertook to rebuke persons for all sorts of moral or ecclesiastical offenses, and often encouraged the civil government to fine or to imprison them. The whole process was certainly too highhanded for our modern age. But a famous visitor from Scotland, John Knox, seeing the high moral tone of the community, called Geneva "the most perfect school of Christ that ever was in the earth since the days of the apostles."

Calvin had very definite ideas about civil government also. God is God of the state or nation, and the state must be guided by his word. This does not mean that the church has authority over the state; rather, both are directly under God. The state should protect and support a true church, but should not interfere in its internal affairs. Calvin certainly did not teach religious liberty as we know it today, but his resistance to interference by the state in church life did hasten the coming of religious liberty.

Because God has appointed governments, Christians must obey them, Calvin said, except only when they command us to do what is contrary to God's revealed will. In that case Christians must refuse to obey, whatever the penalty. Individual citizens may never revolt even against a wicked government. But a part of the government (like Parliament, for example) may lead a revolt against an evil ruler. By teaching that only God is to be obeyed unconditionally, Calvin contributed greatly, even if unintentionally, to the rise of democracy. Reformed and Presbyterian Christians in France, the Netherlands, Britain, America, and other lands would later go much farther in this direction.

Calvin was interested in the total life of the community. He developed education on both the elementary and higher levels, climaxing in the Geneva Academy which opened in 1559. He considered learning closely related to Christian life. The business life of Geneva too claimed some of his attention. He encouraged the weaving industry. Differing from theologians of the Middle Ages, he recognized the right of moneylenders to charge interest on their loans. More than most church leaders of his day he understood the businessman's viewpoint and needs, but he insisted on the duty of the church to speak out against and to punish economic sins.

Christian worship for Calvin receives its distinctive character from the word of God and from the fact that God is entirely spiritual and nonmaterial. Worship is the united act of a disciplined congregation receiving God's word and giving itself to God in praise and obedience. The emphasis is on mind and conscience and away from symbols and appeals to the senses. Singing of psalms amid such solemnity and fervor proved deeply moving. Calvin retained a liturgy for Sunday morning worship, including read prayers along with free prayer. He also prepared liturgical forms for Baptism, Communion, marriage, and the visitation of the sick. Many Presbyterians today who are reacting against the almost slovenly simplicity of nineteenth-century worship are finding valuable suggestions regarding worship in Calvin and in the early Reformed churches.

Like all mortals, Calvin was not without serious faults. He was high-strung and irritable, on occasion carried away by uncontrollable temper. His opinions were sometimes ungenerous. He was reserved, but not cold. But his faults were more than overbalanced by virtues that were more solid than glamorous. His personal life was one of incessant mental toil. While still a university student, he permanently undermined his health by overstudy. Throughout life he was bothered with indigestion and severe headaches. But the resolute mind forced the incompetent body. He rose daily at five or six A.M. His few physical recreations, such as quoits, were brief and infrequent. His time was almost entirely devoted to study, authorship, preaching, consultation, correspondence, and administration. He died at the age of fifty-four, but not before he had completed a magnificent service for the Master, whom he served so wholeheartedly.

He gave himself and his life to God freely and unreservedly. He took the little town of Geneva and made it a center of influence of the Reformed faith. In its churches and schools pastors were trained who carried the freedom and truth of the gospel over Europe. Refugees and visitors from England, Scotland, France, Italy, Germany, and the Netherlands came to Geneva, sat at the feet of Calvin for a time, and then returned to their homelands resolved to overthrow church tyranny and to dispel darkness. The tribute paid to Calvin

by the Little Council of Geneva shortly after his death was richly
deserved: "God gave him a character of great majesty." In the coming chapters we shall watch the growth of the seed that, at the command of God, John Calvin and like-minded leaders had planted and
watered.

CHAPTER III

The Presbyterians on the Continent of Europe

The Huguenots of France. Within a surprisingly short time after Luther had posted his theses in 1517, the religious issue became the chief concern throughout Europe. The new Protestant doctrines were circulated everywhere by the help of the recently invented printing presses. The question in every country was this: Would men stand by the old Catholic Church or would they follow the Protestant Reformers and reject it?

France, the near neighbor of Germany and Switzerland, could not ignore the problem. The first Protestant congregation was organized in that land in an unusual way in 1555. La Ferrière, at whose house a group of Christians was meeting, desired his child to be baptized. As there was no minister available, the assembled Christians promptly organized themselves into a little church and elected a pastor, elders, and deacons. The baptism was then administered.

Four years later there were enough Protestant congregations in France to organize the first synod of the French Reformed Church. It adopted a confession of faith drafted by John Calvin, of Geneva, who, from across the Swiss border, guided the destinies of French Protestantism during its early years. This same synod also adopted a book of discipline that laid the foundations for a more fully developed Presbyterianism than that of Geneva itself, with four levels of judicatories: "consistories" (sessions), "colloquies" (presbyteries), "provincial synods" (synods), and a "National Synod" (General Assembly). This system of ascending courts, found everywhere

27

today in fully developed Presbyterianism, offers the advantage of much local freedom combined with a high degree of central unity.

The remarkable growth of the French Protestants, who were known as Huguenots, aroused the bitter opposition of their religious and political enemies. About sixty were massacred in cold blood one Sunday as they were going to church in the little town of Vassy. This opened a religious war that, with brief interruptions, tore the country for the next thirty years.

The Synod of Rochelle, at which 2,150 Huguenot churches were reported, was the high-water mark of French Presbyterianism. The next year, 1572, the Huguenots received a terrible blow. The Catholic sister of the king of France was marrying the leading Protestant prince, later known as Henry of Navarre. Catholics and Protestants assembled from far and near to celebrate the wedding that seemed to promise an end to the religious wars. Hardly were the celebrations over when the king's mother, unnerved by the failure of an attempt to assassinate one of the Protestant leaders, persuaded the king to order a general massacre of all Protestants in Paris. This took place on St. Bartholomew's Day, August 24, 1572. The butchery spread over France until more than 30,000 Huguenots had been slaughtered.

By a strange turn of fortune the political leader of the Protestants, Henry of Navarre, became heir to the throne of France. With the flippant jest that France was worth a Mass, he turned Catholic and was crowned king. Though he had lightly renounced his religion, he did not forget his old Protestant friends, for in 1598 there was issued with his approval the famous Edict of Nantes, granting liberty of worship to Protestants with a few specified limitations. The edict gave the Huguenots a much-needed breathing spell. From religious wars and other causes, the number of their congregations had been reduced by two thirds in the quarter century preceding the edict.

Henry's grandson, Louis XIV, determined to destroy Protestantism in France. In the houses of the Huguenots he quartered soldiers, who treated their hosts with the coarsest brutality. In 1685, he revoked the Edict of Nantes. Thousands of the Huguenots emigrated, many of them skilled workers who, entering England, Holland, Germany, Ireland, and America, permanently enriched these countries with the industrial arts that they took with them.

Many of the persecuted Huguenots fled to the Cévennes Mountains in France where their boy general, Jean Cavalier, for three years led them successfully against the best troops of France. At last, in 1715, Louis XIV officially declared the "heresy" exterminated; but in that very year the Huguenots, in an old stone quarry near Nîmes, France, were organizing "The Church in the Desert." Within a few years assemblies of 3,000 were not uncommon.

With the coming of the French Revolution in 1789, a great anti-religious wave swept France, closing all churches, Catholic and Protestant alike. Six years later the Huguenots were granted freedom to worship God according to their own consciences, a privilege that they have enjoyed from that day to the present. Pastor Bersier, a Presbyterian minister of Paris, spoke truly to the Pan-Presbyterian Council in 1888, when he said: "I represent a great Presbyterian Church—I may say the greatest, when I think of what it has suffered for the cause of Christ and human liberty. And though we are small now, we may say that our poverty has been the riches of many nations." All honor to the heroic Huguenots of France, who so courageously gave up wealth, homeland, and life itself at the call of their Master!

The "Beggars" of the Netherlands. At the time of the Protestant Reformation, modern Holland and Belgium were a single country, known as "the Netherlands," ruled by the king of Spain. The Reformation doctrines entered the Netherlands very early, two Protestants being martyred there within six years after the Reformation had started in Germany. It was, however, Calvin and the Reformed, as distinguished from the Lutheran, form of Protestantism that exercised the determining influence on the Netherlands.

In 1555, Philip II became ruler of the Netherlands. He soon became unpopular there by his tyranny over the nobles, and by his persecution of Protestants, a policy that had a damaging effect on the flourishing economic life of the country.

The land was growing restless under this iron rule, and in 1566 five hundred nobles petitioned Philip's regent, the Duchess of Parma, for justice. This formidable paper made the Duchess highly nervous, but one of her counselors, who was standing at her side, sought to hearten her with the words, "Madam, are you afraid of a pack of beggars?"

The Protestant leaders proudly assumed the name "Beggars." Failing to secure peaceable redress, bands of Protestants in the same year invaded the old churches, smashed beautiful windows, and broke images, statues, crucifixes, and altars. It cannot be denied that the act was utterly lawless, but King Philip exacted a terrible penalty. The next year he sent the Duke of Alva to the Netherlands with ten thousand troops, who soon executed some eighteen hundred persons.

In this dark hour God raised up a leader for his persecuted people in the person of William the Silent, prince of Orange. In one of the most desperate struggles in history, extending over a period of forty years, William and his successors succeeded in freeing the northern Netherlands (modern Holland) from the Spanish yoke, gaining thereby the right to worship God according to their own consciences.

In 1574 the tide turned in favor of the Dutch. The Spanish were besieging the city of Leyden. Food was so scarce that cats, dogs, and even rats were eaten. William had courageously broken the dikes, and, after a long delay, the winds brought the waters of the North Sea to the very walls of Leyden. The Dutch ships relieved the city. The grateful population went in a body to the cathedral to pour out their heartfelt thanksgiving to God. William rewarded the fortitude of Leyden by founding a university there a few months later.

Five years after the relief of Leyden the northern provinces of the Netherlands, which were now prevailingly Protestant, formed the Union of Utrecht, from which sprang modern Holland. Within two years this Union declared its independence of Spain. The southern provinces of the Netherlands returned to their allegiance to Spain and to Catholicism. They later became modern Belgium.

William of Orange, against the wishes of the Reformed Church, insisted on tolerating other churches. Thus Holland, which was a great center of trade and banking, became a refuge for people of many lands who were persecuted for their religion. In other nations, too, Reformed and Presbyterian churchmen would give up their earlier ideal, inherited from the Middle Ages, of imposing their faith by government power and would contribute mightily to the newer and more democratic ideal of religious liberty.

After having successfully resisted persecutions from without, the Church of the Netherlands was troubled by controversy within. Amid the prosperous business life of the country, some theologians, led by Jacobus Arminius, professor of theology at the new University of Leyden, began to hold views about man's goodness and moral ability that differed from the earlier Reformed emphasis on God's grace. The whole country became sharply divided, and a synod was convened at Dort in 1618 to settle the dispute. There were twenty-eight delegates from foreign lands, in addition to those from the Netherlands. The synod rejected the doctrines of Arminius, but in endorsing Calvinistic teaching about God's grace made it narrower and more speculative, as often happens in controversy. Before the end of the century, some Reformed Church theologians, reacting against the Synod of Dort, were emphasizing God's love for all men, a tendency that was carried much farther in the nineteenth and twentieth centuries.

The Church of the Netherlands was a powerful influence in spreading the Presbyterian faith. Huguenots from France, Puritans from England, Covenanters from Scotland, fleeing from persecution in their homelands, found welcome and shelter in the Netherlands with its religious freedom. As a result of their contact with the churches of this land, they returned home more enthusiastic than ever in their Presbyterian convictions. Dutch colonial expansion during the seventeenth century also had the effect of enlarging the Presbyterian influence of the country. Dutch colonists carried their faith with them to the Dutch Indies, America, and South Africa.

Holland today occupies a high place in the economic and cultural life of the world. Its flourishing Reformed churches occupy a distinguished and influential position in the Presbyterian world family of churches.

Presbyterianism Elsewhere on the European Continent. Presbyterianism met with its greatest acceptance in Switzerland, the Netherlands, Britain, and America. We have just discussed France and the Netherlands; we shall view Great Britain and America in later chapters. Here we briefly trace the story of Presbyterianism in some of the other lands of Europe.

In *Germany* the Lutheran, as distinguished from the Reformed, branch of Protestantism dominated from the earliest days. Since

World War II those holding the Reformed faith in Germany number less than half a million.

In *Bohemia* (*Czechoslovakia* today), a century before Luther's time, John Hus had protested against the corruptions of the Roman Church. In the latter part of the sixteenth century many of his spiritual descendants accepted Calvin's views. By the end of the century the Protestants numbered about four fifths of the entire population of Bohemia. But disaster lay just ahead. As a result of their unsuccessful revolt against their Catholic king, persecution arose that reduced their numbers by three fourths. Though toleration came later, Presbyterians have remained a small minority in this land. At the end of World War I, with the erection of Czechoslovakia as a separate nation with universal religious liberty, the future of Presbyterianism in this land appeared more hopeful. But the domination of the land by Communist Russia at the end of World War II made prospects less clear.

In *Hungary* the Lutheran faith, which had entered first, was early replaced by the Reformed, or Calvinistic. By 1600 the Protestants of the country were in a majority, but unusually heavy persecutions that came in the following century cut their numbers by at least a half. As a result of World War I, Hungary lost two thirds of its territory, and after World War II the land came under Russian domination, but the Reformed faith continues as a vigorous minority movement.

Greece reports some 2,000 Reformed members, and *Yugoslavia,* 25,000. *Rumania,* under Russian domination, reports 380,000 Reformed. *Austria, Italy, Spain, Portugal, Belgium,* and *Poland* are prevailingly Catholic countries today. The six together report less than 45,000 Presbyterians.

The present chapter has given a very brief survey of Presbyterianism on the Continent of Europe. It took deep root in the Netherlands, and flourishes there today; but in other countries of Continental Europe, though it entered some of them early, it proved less successful numerically. We turn now to the countries that became and still are the principal strongholds of Presbyterianism—Great Britain (especially Scotland and northern Ireland) and America.

CHAPTER IV

The Presbyterians in Scotland and Ireland

Scotland. For more than three hundred years the chief center of Presbyterianism in Europe has been Scotland. The hero of the Reformation in Scotland was John Knox. In one of our first glimpses of his public life, we find him with a company of fellow Christians in the Castle of St. Andrews, which was being besieged by the French. A preacher of this little band, John Rough, "called" Knox to the Christian ministry with these words: "In the name of God, and of his Sone Jesus Christ, and in the name of these that presentlie calles yow by my mouth, I charge yow that ye refuise not this holy vocatioun." Though he fully realized the perils involved, Knox was "not disobedient unto the heavenly vision."

The French captured St. Andrews, and Knox as a prisoner was condemned to row in the French galleys for nineteen months. This was followed by an exile of almost twelve years in England, France, Switzerland, and Germany, with only one brief visit to Scotland.

Knox finally returned to his native land in 1559. When he had left about twelve years before, the Protestants had been only a small minority. Now the whole land was seething with discontent, ripe for reformation. After some fighting, in which valuable assistance was received from Elizabeth, the Protestant queen of England, the French, who had usurped control of the country, were driven out. The Scottish Parliament which met in 1560 abolished Catholicism, and set up as the religion of the land what soon became fully developed Presbyterianism.

The struggle seemed to be ended, but it was not, for the next year Mary Stuart, the young queen of Scotland, returned to take over the rule of her kingdom after a long sojourn in France. A woman of great personal charm, she was officially committed to the abandoned Roman Catholic faith. A contest between two such leaders as Knox and Queen Mary was inevitable. In less than a month after Mary's arrival, Knox thundered from the pulpit of St. Giles' Church, Edinburgh, that one Mass "was more fearful to him then yif ten thousand armed enemyes war landed in any pairte of the Realme." The new queen could not ignore this public challenge to her policies, and summoned Knox to a private interview. On at least five dramatic occasions these two antagonists, the stern reformer and the bewitching queen, stood face to face. Knox expressed his opinion of the queen to some friends: "Yf thair be not in hir . . . a proud mynd, a crafty witt, and ane indurat hearte against God and his treuth, my judgment faileth me." Her opinion of Knox, though on different grounds, was every bit as hostile.

To Knox's consternation, the queen seemed gradually to be winning the country back to Catholicism, when a serious moral scandal in her private life brought her into disgrace and necessitated her flight to England, where she was later executed by Queen Elizabeth.

Scottish Presbyterianism, under Knox's leadership, had succeeded in maintaining its existence against Catholic reaction. After Knox's death, under the leadership of Andrew Melville, it faced the further necessity of defending itself against Episcopalianism, or the system of government by bishops.

In 1603, James VI of Scotland became king of England also, under the title of James I. From that day to the present, England and Scotland have been under the same ruler, though for more than a century each country retained its separate Parliament. Intensely autocratic, James bitterly opposed Presbyterianism because of its democratic tendencies, and sought to transform it gradually into Episcopalianism.

Charles I, son and successor of James, carried his father's policy farther. In 1637 he ordered a form of worship, more Catholic than the English Prayer Book, to be introduced into Scotland. When this service was used in St. Giles' Church, Edinburgh, legend says that Janet Geddes picked up the stool on which she was sitting, and threw it at the clergyman's head, crying out: "Fause loon, dost thou say Mass at my lug [ear]!" Others threw stools and Bibles. When the bishop sought to quiet the crowd, there were loud cries of, "A pope, a pope, down with him!" Charles, when he heard of the disturbance, was furious, but Scotland was now thoroughly aroused.

The next year great numbers of ministers, nobles, gentry, and peasants gathered in old Greyfriars' Church and agreed to a "National Covenant," pledging to defend the doctrine and discipline of their beloved Church of Scotland. A Scottish General Assembly which met soon afterward rejected all the Episcopalian elements that James and Charles had been introducing, and returned to original Presbyterianism. Charles twice sent an army against Scotland, but twice withdrew, when he found Scottish soldiers ready to resist him.

From this time on Charles had trouble enough at home. Civil war between him and the English Parliament broke out, and in 1643 the Scottish and English Parliaments agreed to a "Solemn League and Covenant" allying them against the king. Six years later, contrary to the desire of most of the Scots, King Charles was executed. Oliver Cromwell ruled as "Protector," but after Cromwell's death the country restored the monarchy by welcoming back to the throne Charles II, son of the executed Charles I.

Profiting nothing by his father's experience, Charles II at once set himself to transforming Scottish Presbyterianism into Episcopalianism. The Scots were particularly embittered by the fact that many of the king's most zealous agents were former Scottish Presbyterians. Rather than submit to the new regulations, four hundred Scottish pastors and many of their parishioners worshiped outdoors, with some of their own number stationed as armed guards for protection. On several occasions the king's soldiers attacked bands of armed civilians, usually defeating them.

The most uncompromising resisters of Charles II were the so-called "Covenanters," who charged that Charles was a usurper for violating the National Covenant and the Solemn League and Covenant which they regarded as divine-human covenants and as the social contracts that were now the permanent foundation of the government of Scotland. In thus declaring open war against the king, the Covenanters became a heroic but dwindling remnant.

In the midst of this struggle Charles II died, and was succeeded by his Roman Catholic brother, James II. The English Parliament, fearing lest James would reintroduce Roman Catholicism, invited William of Orange, ruler of the Netherlands, and his wife, Mary, to take the throne of England. This was known as the "Glorious Revolution" of 1688.

William III had been reared in the Reformed (Presbyterian) Church of the Netherlands and was therefore sympathetic to the Presbyterian ideals of his new Scottish subjects. A year after the Revolution the Scottish Parliament declared Presbyterianism to be the official religion of Scotland. "Lay patronage"—whereby certain wealthy laymen appointed the pastors for the various churches, often forcing altogether unworthy men on congregations—was abolished. But the Covenanters refused to be a part of the official Presbyterian Church because the new monarchs had not reaffirmed the Covenants, which the Covenanters considered permanent and which, they felt, should be "renewed," that is, reaffirmed, from time to time. In 1876 most of them united with the Free Church of Scotland.

Shortly after William's death, lay patronage was again forced on the Scottish Church. As a result of this and other causes, some who became known as the "Seceders" or "Secession Church" withdrew in 1733 to form the Associate Presbytery. Like the Covenanters before them, the Seceders emphasized "renewing the Covenants," but in a way that was spiritual and nonpolitical—a kind of individual and group rededication to Christian faith and life. This practice of covenanting contributed much to the spiritual life of the early Seceders. In 1847 the Secession Church and the Relief Church, which had also withdrawn because of lay patronage, came together to form the United Presbyterian Church of Scotland. This union was a landmark, because from about that time Presbyterians all over the world became much more active in uniting than in dividing.

But, unhappily, the old grievance of lay patronage was to cause still further division in the Scottish Church. In the great Disruption of 1843, Dr. Thomas Chalmers and other notable ministers led out of the Church of Scotland over a third of its ministers and elders and all but one of its missionaries. The new organization was called the Free Church of Scotland. It was a courageous act, for those who went out automatically sacrificed their share of the financial support which the government gave the established Church of Scotland. At last, in 1874, the old bone of contention, lay patronage, was removed, and the congregations of the Church of Scotland also were granted the right of electing their own pastors.

In the year 1900, by an act of enlightened statesmanship, the Free Church of Scotland merged with the United Presbyterian Church of Scotland to form the United Free Church of Scotland. This still left a number of much smaller Presbyterian bodies in the land, but these two—the Church of Scotland and the United Free Church—now constituted the preponderating bulk of Scotch Presbyterianism. In 1929 these two merged under the name "Church of Scotland." With a membership of nearly 1,300,000, this new merged church is second in size only to the United Presbyterian Church in the United States of America among the Presbyterian Churches of the world.

Ireland. The people of Ulster, the northern section of Ireland, are commonly known as "Scotch-Irish," and to the story of Presbyterianism among them we now turn. This is a subject of great interest to every American Presbyterian, in view of the fact that the emigrants from northern Ireland have deeply influenced American Presbyterianism.

Several years before James I came to the throne of England a powerful rebellion broke out in Ulster. The rebels were defeated, and their lands were declared forfeited to the crown. When James I, who had become king of England in 1603, invited colonists from Scotland and England to settle these confiscated lands, the Scots responded so enthusiastically that very soon the population of northern Ireland was quite Scottish, hence the name of these people, Scotch-Irish.

The English Church, at this time Episcopalian, enjoyed official supremacy in Ireland, but felt overwhelmed by the deluge of Scottish newcomers, who were a mixture of Presbyterians and irreligious renegades. The Episcopal officials were therefore glad to secure the services of Presbyterian ministers from Scotland to work among the new arrivals. A great revival which came soon afterward confirmed the Scotch-Irish in their Presbyterianism, and defeated the original hope of the officials gradually to wean them away from Presbyterianism to Episcopalianism. Charles I, king of England, unsuccessfully endeavored by persecution to destroy Irish Presbyterianism, even imprisoning many and pulling down the homes of others.

As might well be supposed, the native Irish, who were enthusiastic Roman Catholics, resented this unwelcome intrusion of Scottish and English settlers, and rose up in revolt in 1641, massacring great numbers of the Protestant immigrants. Scotland, retaining a parental interest in its sons who had migrated to Ireland, sent 10,000 troops to suppress the insurrection. As the Scotch-Irish Presbyterian ministers and the Episcopal clergy had almost all been either slain or driven out by the rioters, the only clergymen now left in Ulster were the Presbyterian chaplains of the Scottish troops. For soldiers, these Scots were remarkably religious, for each regiment was organized as a church congregation, having over it a session of chaplain and soldier-elders. In 1642 the first presbytery ever formed in Ireland was organized out of these regimental church sessions. Civilian Presbyterian ministers soon were added to the number of army chaplains, and within less than twenty years there were eighty Presbyterian congregations, with 100,000 members in Ulster.

Charles II, who came to the English throne at the Restoration of the monarchy after Oliver Cromwell's "Protectorate," did all in his power to destroy Presbyterianism in Ireland, just as we have observed that he did in Scotland. He sent troops to disperse the Irish synod at Ballymena, and offered Presbyterian ministers the choice of becoming Episcopalians or of being debarred from their pulpits. It was their faithfulness at this time which saved northern Ireland for Presbyterianism. Within a few years these ejected ministers were preaching in improvised churches to enthusiastic audiences.

James II, who succeeded his brother Charles II, was a Catholic, and therefore had no zeal for making Presbyterians into Episcopalians. Instead, he gave religious freedom to all non-Episcopalian groups, including both Presbyterians and Roman Catholics. James also replaced Protestant army officers in Ireland with Roman Catholic.

Probably as a result of James's policy of placing the Irish army under control of Roman Catholics, a rumor spread that a massacre of Protestants was being planned. Consequently, when the government troops commanded by Lord Antrim, a Roman Catholic, sought to enter the city of Derry in Ulster, the inhabitants, encouraged by the counsel of a Presbyterian minister named James Gordon, closed the gates of the city. A desperate siege of more than a hundred days followed, in which food became so scarce that rats were eaten. But relief came at last to the gallant defenders, who had entertained no thought of surrender. Their exploit is esteemed as one of Ulster's most honored memories.

By the Glorious Revolution of 1688, Parliament dethroned the Roman Catholic, James II, and chose the Protestant, William of Orange, to succeed him. The Battle of the Boyne is another celebrated event of Ulster history, for here William of Orange, leading a Protestant army, decisively defeated the ousted king, James II, at the head of his loyal Irish Roman Catholic supporters, and saved Ulster for Protestantism. King William was a Presbyterian at heart, and under his rule Presbyterianism in northern Ireland flourished.

The persecution of Irish Presbyterians by Charles II helped to lay solid foundations for Presbyterianism in America, for great numbers of the persecuted sought refuge in the New World. In 1683, in answer to the request for a minister for the Scotch-Irish immigrants recently settled in America, the Presbytery of Laggan, in Ireland, sent Rev. Francis Makemie, who is commonly considered the father of organized American Presbyterianism. In 1729, and for many years thereafter, as a result of further discontent in the homeland, a steady stream of Scotch-Irish flowed to America. The loss to Ireland was great, but the gain to the cause of Presbyterianism in the New World was almost beyond calculation, as will be seen in later chapters.

Just as political persecution was ending for the Irish Presbyterians, following the Glorious Revolution of 1688, internal doctrinal disputes arose. Low views of Christ's divinity, known as Arianism and Unitarianism, spread among the clergy. The conservative Secession Church of Scotland founded a work in Ireland which soon became known as the Secession Synod, and exercised strong influence against the new doctrinal views. The old Irish Church, known as the Synod of Ulster, underwent a conservative reaction at this time too, and required that all candidates for the ministry subscribe the Westminster Confession of Faith. The two principal Presbyterian churches in

Ireland—the Synod of Ulster and the Secession Synod—were now at one in conservative faith and united in 1840 under the name, the General Assembly of the Presbyterian Church in Ireland.

This combination of denominations laid solid foundations for the strong Irish Presbyterianism of today. In 1840 the Irish Presbyterians started a foreign missionary enterprise. Not until 1892 was instrumental music sanctioned for worship, and non-Biblical hymns were not permitted until 1895.

One friendly commentator has said of this church: "It may be safely said that the Presbyterian Church of Ireland is one of the most thoroughly orthodox, consistently conservative, and healthfully active of all the churches in the great brotherhood of like faith and order." Before we see what these doughty sons of Erin did for Presbyterianism in the New World, let us pause to review the story of Presbyterianism in England and Wales.

CHAPTER V

The Presbyterians in England, Wales, and the British Dominions

England. One of the most creative forces in English history was Puritanism, a movement in which Presbyterians played a very important part. William Tyndale, whose English translation of the New Testament was published in 1525 and who was martyred eleven years later, was an early Puritan.

Meanwhile King Henry VIII, who was not in sympathy with these early Puritan tendencies, in 1534 persuaded the English Parliament to declare the Church of England entirely independent of the pope. But Henry tried to keep the church as close as possible to medieval Catholic beliefs and customs in other respects. Under Henry's son, the boy king Edward VI, many mildly Protestant doctrines and practices were introduced that were to contribute to the Church of England much of its modern Anglican character. Edward's sister, Mary, who succeeded him on the throne, was an enthusiastic Roman Catholic and persecuted Protestants, some of whom fled to Calvin at Geneva and to other Protestant centers on the European continent.

Elizabeth I came to the throne of England in 1558. She was "Protestant" in rejecting the pope's rule over the Church of England; but she was "Catholic" in desiring, like her father, Henry VIII, to retain as much as possible of the medieval Catholic doctrines, ceremonies, and organization.

This did not satisfy the Puritans, however. Many of them, becoming acquainted with Reformers on the Continent during their recent exile, had been strengthened in their desire for thoroughgoing

Protestantism. Early in Elizabeth's reign the Puritans received their name from their desire to restore what they considered the "purity" of New Testament worship by discarding the old Catholic vestments for clergy and Catholic ceremonies. In their zeal for a simplified worship, many Puritans went far beyond the practice of the Reformed Churches of the Continent, and bequeathed to nineteenth-century America a worship service that by then had become quite bare. Most of the Puritans in Elizabeth's day had no thought of leaving the Church of England; rather, they desired to remain within it and to carry farther all along the line the revolt against Catholicism, which, they felt, had not gone nearly far enough.

Many, though not all, of the Puritans were Presbyterians; that is, in addition to desiring a simpler form of worship, they felt that the church should be governed by ministers and elders, not by a higher order of clergy known as bishops. In 1572 an *Admonition to Parliament,* advocating definitely Presbyterian principles, was drafted. At about the same time a few skeleton "presbyteries" composed of ministers and laymen tried to function informally within the Church of England. But Queen Elizabeth resisted every alteration. The leader of the Presbyterians, Dr. Thomas Cartwright, had already been removed from his professorship at Cambridge University. An Act of Uniformity prescribed the ritual of worship for every congregation. Many ministers who refused to conform to it were removed from their pulpits or imprisoned. It is estimated that, during Elizabeth's reign, a third of the English clergy suffered penalties of one kind or other.

Elizabeth died in 1603, and James VI of Scotland succeeded her as James I of England. At a conference the next year James dismayed the Puritans by declaring that a Scottish presbytery "agreeth as well with a monarchy as God and the devil." After hearing the Puritans further, James said, "If this be all your party have to say, I will make them conform, or I will harry them out of the land." True to his threat, James, throughout his reign, made every effort to force Puritans to conform to the semi-Catholic ritual of the English Church.

Charles I carried the persecution of Puritans even farther than did his father, James I. Puritans fleeing from his harsh treatment founded Massachusetts Bay Colony in America. Charles's tyrannies of many

sorts brought about armed warfare between him and Parliament, resulting in the victory of Parliament's army, led by Oliver Cromwell,
and the execution of Charles in 1649.

For a time the Presbyterian wing of the Puritan party dominated
the situation. In 1642, Parliament abolished episcopacy, and con-
voked the Westminster Assembly of Divines, which met in 1643, to
advise them how to proceed in reconstructing the Church of England.
The Westminster Assembly was controlled by men of Presbyterian
convictions, and the documents which this body composed—the
Larger and Shorter Catechisms, the Westminster Confession of Faith,
and the Directory of Public Worship—are in our own day, with slight
modifications, the official doctrinal and liturgical standards of the
great majority of Presbyterian churches the world over. Presbyterianism seemed to have won completely, for Parliament soon made it
the official form of government of the Church of England.

The Westminster Standards were based on the covenant theology
which, with variations, Puritans had long held. God entered into
a covenant with fallen man, offering him salvation in Christ upon
condition of man's faith. This covenant theology resembled and
strengthened the social-contract political thought that the Puritans
had inherited from ancient and medieval times. Men, said the social-
contract theory, enter into a contract with a king to rule over them.
The theory has democratic, even radical implications, for it teaches
that if the king violates the terms of the contract and becomes a
tyrant, he may be restrained or even deposed. This goes far beyond
the teaching of Calvin. The social-contract view, reinforced by the
Puritans' covenant theology, and drawing strength also from more
secular sources, was the foundation for the Puritans' revolt against
Charles I, for the Glorious Revolution of 1688, and later still for the
American Revolution. The contribution of Puritanism toward the
development of democracy in the modern world has been almost
beyond calculation.

But the victory of the Presbyterians in Parliament soon proved to
be more apparent than real. The Puritans were much divided among
themselves, ecclesiastically, politically, and socially. They had been
able to act together against the king and the Anglicans, but when
they came to power their differences caused them to fall apart. Some

of the Puritans were satisfied with the episcopal form of church government; many preferred the presbyterian; others preferred the independent, or congregational; the more radical sects desired to weaken church government still farther. There were corresponding political differences among the Puritans. Episcopalian, Presbyterian, and some Independent Puritans desired to retain monarchy, but with constitutional controls; whereas some Independents and most of the sects wished to abolish monarchy and to set up a republic. Though Parliament was controlled by the Presbyterians, the army was controlled by the Independents and the sects. And in days of upheaval and change, the real power of the country was in the hands of the army and not of the Parliament. Thus we see the strange fact that, though Presbyterianism had recently been declared by Parliament to be the official religion of England, it never was given a trial on a wide scale in the nation as a whole.

When, after Cromwell's death, the monarchy and Anglicanism were restored in 1660, Presbyterians once more found themselves a persecuted minority. All clergymen were required to become Episcopalians within three months or to resign their pastorates. Over two thousand ministers—many of them Presbyterians—gave up their livings rather than their convictions.

In the Glorious Revolution which occurred in 1688 the political ideals of the Presbyterians and other right-wing Puritans triumphed, because William and Mary, created sovereigns by act of Parliament, would necessarily be, together with their successors, under the control of Parliament. The Toleration Act of 1689 granted toleration to all non-Episcopalian Protestant groups. This was a first decisive step toward the ideal of religious liberty previously held by the more radical Puritans and now being adopted also by the heirs of the moderate Puritans, including the Presbyterians. Thus, though the Puritans had failed to gain control of the Church of England, their political ideals contributed heavily to the transformation of the English-speaking world. Office in the government and education at the leading universities were closed to Dissenters, as the former Puritans were now called, but they became leaders in the business life of England, which expanded vastly in the eighteenth century. By then, however, Dissenters were unfortunately abandoning the moral restraint on economic sins that Calvin and the early Reformed leaders had tried to provide.

The eighteenth century was an extremely unfortunate period for English Presbyterianism. At the Revolution of 1688 there had been more than five hundred Presbyterian churches, but a century later only about three hundred. Efforts of Presbyterians and Congregationalists in the 1690's to join forces, known as the "Heads of Agreement," did encourage the two groups to co-operate in the American colonies, but these were not effective in England. The civil government abolished the higher Presbyterian judicatories of presbytery and synod. Low views of Christ's divinity, known as Arianism and Unitarianism, were widely held. Another reason for the eighteenth-century decline was an inadequately trained ministry, the leading theological educational institutions being open only to members of the Church of England. Though a remnant survived, much of English Presbyterianism went to pieces at this time. Many joined other non-Anglican churches, especially the Independents, while others became Anglicans, and some abandoned the Christian church entirely. Those who remained under the Presbyterian banner were so decreased in numbers, loose in organization, and vague in beliefs as to be almost negligible as a force in the life of England.

English Presbyterianism was saved by the Scots. Even in the eighteenth century, Presbyterianism in the three northern counties of England had been more successfully maintained than in the rest of the country, due to a steady supply of Scottish-trained ministers for the pulpits and Scottish-born worshipers for the pews. There were also a number of flourishing congregations of Scottish Presbyterians in London. These strong centers had been further strengthened by the Methodist revival under John Wesley.

In the nineteenth century renewed immigration of Scots into England further resuscitated English Presbyterianism. In 1836 the Church of Scotland organized a synod in England which remained under the control of the Scottish General Assembly. When the Disruption divided the Scottish Church seven years later, most of its English synod went with the Scottish Free Church. A little later a synod was organized in England under the General Assembly of the United Presbyterian Church of Scotland. In 1876 these two Scottish synods in England united to form the Presbyterian Church of England. Thus once more, thanks to Scottish influence, England had a flourishing, even though small, Presbyterian Church of its own. At the close of the last century this church founded Westminster College at Cambridge University, and in 1921 first organized a General Assembly as its highest court. This church is disappointingly small, reporting a little less than 70,000 members, but it is built on solid foundations and gives promise of an assured future in this great nation.

Wales. Wales, the little land on the west border of England, small as it is, has a Presbyterian Church more than twice as large as that of England.

In 1735 a great religious revival broke out in Wales as a result of the labors of Howell Harris, an Oxford-educated lay evangelist. This was before the Methodist revival movement under Whitefield and Wesley had got under way. Within four years he had organized thirty groups, which he called, not churches, but "societies." Three years later these societies held their first meeting of the General Association. The powerful preaching of the English revivalist George Whitefield also had an inspiring influence on the Welsh movement soon after it had started.

It was not the intention of these early Welsh leaders to found a new church. The converts attended the meetings of the societies, but received Communion in the Church of England. The Church of England, however, soon showed hostility to the new movement, and attendance at the meetings of the societies was punished with fines and imprisonment. In view of this unfriendly attitude, when the revival movement needed more workers its only available solution was to ordain its own ministers. Thus in 1811 was organized the Calvinistic Methodist Church of Wales.

The new church was quite truly Presbyterian in its form of government. Over the local societies (corresponding to our congregations) were monthly meetings (corresponding to our presbyteries). A few years later two quarterly associations (corresponding to our synods), one for North Wales and one for South Wales, were added. Over this, a little later still, was erected a General Assembly for all of Wales. This vigorous Welsh church, like most of its sister Presbyterian churches, holds to the theological system associated with the name of John Calvin. It maintains two colleges, home and foreign missionary enterprises, and evangelistic halls in a number of cities. The work is thoroughly Welsh, the Welsh language rather than English being used in a large number of the congregations. The Presbyterian Church of Wales today reports over 150,000 members.

Canada. Let us round out our view of the chief centers of British Presbyterianism by brief visits to the four British dominions, Canada, Australia, New Zealand, and South Africa.

In 1713 Great Britain received from France what is now Nova Scotia, and in 1763 all of Canada. Presbyterianism in Scotland was at this time much divided, and several of these fragmentary Scottish denominations each founded work in Canada. The result was that by 1845 there were five separate sects of Presbyterians in the eastern part of Canada, as we now call the land, and three more in the western part. A series of mergers in the next twenty-three years happily reduced the number to four. Of the four, the Church of Scotland had one group in both East and West, while the United and Free Churches had union enterprises in both East and West. In 1875 the four came together to form a single denomination, the Presbyterian Church in Canada.

An unprecedented action was taken when the Presbyterian Church of Canada merged with the Methodist and Congregational Churches in 1925 to form the United Church of Canada. This noble experiment is prospering, with a membership today of about 900,000. A large body of the Presbyterians declined to enter the union, and continues under the old name, with a membership of about 180,000.

Australia, New Zealand, and South Africa. The island-continent of *Australia* has a Presbyterian Church of more than 100,000 members. *New Zealand,* its neighbor to the southeast, has a Presbyterian Church of about 70,000. Attempts to merge the Presbyterian, Methodist, and Congregationalist Churches in these two countries, respectively, have so far been unsuccessful.

South Africa, originally settled by the Dutch, has flourishing Dutch

Reformed churches with an aggregate membership of nearly 700,000 which are Presbyterian in fact, though not in name. The Presbyterian Church of South Africa, properly so called, is of Scottish origin, and numbers nearly 37,000 members. The native blacks have been organized in a separate Bantu Presbyterian Church of South Africa. Attempts to merge with the Congregationalists have so far proved unsuccessful.

It is encouraging to see the vigor and activity of Presbyterianism in the Anglo-Saxon dominions. The rapid development of these new lands gives encouraging assurance of the further expansion of Presbyterianism as a world-wide force for Christ.

Having now surveyed Presbyterianism in lands abroad, let us turn, in the remaining chapters, to the absorbing story of Presbyterianism in the United States of America.

CHAPTER VI

The Presbytery

The Presbyterian Church in the U.S.A. In 1957 the Presbyterian Church in the U.S.A. and the United Presbyterian Church of North America merged to form the United Presbyterian Church in the U.S.A. Chapters VI-XII, immediately following, will deal with the history of the Presbyterian Church in the U.S.A., and Chapter XIII will treat the history of the United Presbyterian Church of North America.

Presbyterians Come to America. Christopher Columbus discovered America just twenty-five years before Martin Luther started the Protestant Reformation. England was predominantly Protestant by 1607, the date when the first American colony was planted at Jamestown, Virginia. As a result, England's American empire—which before the Revolutionary War extended from Hudson Bay to Florida and westward from the Atlantic Ocean to the Mississippi River, with practically all its population east of the Appalachian Mountains—was destined to be overwhelmingly Protestant.

Great numbers of these earliest American settlers—even those of non-British origin—were not only Protestant but also Presbyterian. For example, among the early immigrants were English Puritans of Presbyterian convictions, Scottish and Scotch-Irish Presbyterians, Huguenots from France, and adherents of the Reformed churches of Switzerland, Germany, and Holland. From the beginning American Presbyterianism had the advantage, and also the problem, of a richly diversified racial origin; and this has been characteristic of it ever since.

[margin handwritten note: From the beginning, American Presbyterianism has shared a richly diversified racial origin.]

Presbyterians in America were not organized into a permanent presbytery until the comparatively late date of 1706. But before this time there were many isolated ministers and congregations with Presbyterian convictions scattered widely over the colonies. Let us visit a very few of these isolated Presbyterian groups in the three geographical areas of New England, the middle colonies, and the southern colonies.

New England. New England was settled by the Pilgrims and other Puritans. The Pilgrims, who landed at Plymouth in 1620, had separated from the Church of England some time before leaving their native land, and had adopted a form of local church government similar to modern Congregationalism. But the Puritans who came to Massachusetts Bay Colony were predominantly those who had never separated from the Church of England, but who had labored to "purify" it from inside, as we saw in Chapter V. Even before leaving England, they had favored a congregationalist type of church government. Congregationalism was soon so strong in New England that it was established by various colonial legislatures, and came to be known as the "Standing Order."

Cotton Mather, a prominent New England Puritan, estimated that of the 21,000 Puritans coming to New England between 1620 and 1640 more than 4,000 held Presbyterian views of church government. But many of these were soon carried along by the tide of Congregationalism; and though Scotch-Irish Presbyterians and some Huguenots later entered New England, the Presbyterians there remained a small minority compared with the prevailing Congregationalists. New England Congregationalists, especially those in Connecticut, maintained a cordial attitude toward Presbyterianism, and when they moved into the middle and southern colonies they usually became Presbyterians.

The Middle Colonies. The middle colonies were, and still are even today, the stronghold of American Presbyterianism. These colonies were founded after the English Civil War and Restoration offered religious toleration, which was an attraction to the Presbyterians who had no New World church establishment of their own. More than sixty years before any permanent presbytery was organized in America, New England Puritans, migrating south to Long Island, organized churches which were, or later became, Presbyterian. In *1640* the 1640's churches were organized at Southold and Southampton. At least eight others were founded on Long Island within the next thirty years. Francis Doughty and Richard Denton were among the earliest Presbyterian ministers to labor here. French Huguenots organized a church on Staten Island in 1685.

Francis Doughty moved on to New York City, then the Dutch "New Amsterdam," where he ministered to a group of Puritans for five years. England acquired New Amsterdam in 1664, and under the autocratic rule of the early English governors of New York, Presbyterianism did not flourish. The Dutch Reformed Church worshiped in the Dutch language, and was unmolested in Long Island and New York. It was really the oldest "Presbyterian" church in these parts, but its organization remained separate from that of the Presbyterian Church properly so called. French Huguenots founded churches in New York in 1683 and 1688.

Puritans from Connecticut and Long Island founded Presbyterian churches in New Jersey also. In 1667 they organized a congregation *1670's.* at Newark, in 1668 one at Elizabeth, in 1680 one at Woodbridge, and in 1692 one at Fairfield. It is estimated that by 1700 there were about ten or fifteen Presbyterian churches in New York and New Jersey of New England Puritan origin, a very important nucleus for the Presbyterianism that was later to be organized. In 1685, Presbyterian "Covenanters" arrived in New Jersey, fleeing from the "killing times" in Scotland.

In 1692 a Presbyterian congregation began to meet in Philadelphia in the "Barbadoes Company Warehouse." Nine years later Jedediah Andrews, a Harvard graduate, was ordained and installed pastor of the First Presbyterian Church of Philadelphia.

The Southern Colonies. Puritans had settled in Virginia too and, when Governor Berkeley persecuted them there, many of them in 1649 moved to Maryland. Soon after 1660 Presbyterian colonists from Scotland and Ireland added to their numbers, forming the material for early Maryland Presbyterianism. Francis Doughty, whom we met in Long Island and New York, came to minister in Maryland in 1650. Matthew Hill, a Presbyterian minister from England, also labored in Maryland. Toward the end of the seventeenth century the Puritan clergy of New England sent missionaries to the Delaware valley, many of whom became pastors of Presbyterian churches in Maryland and Delaware.

Early Presbyterianism was less strong in the southern colonies because Episcopalianism was eventually established by law in all of them, even as Congregationalism was in most of New England. A Virginia law of 1618 punished absentees from the Episcopal Church service by fine and by a night in the stocks. Driven out of Virginia by persecution, some Presbyterians moved to North Carolina as early as 1650, and, a little later, into South Carolina. Immigrants from England, Scotland, and New England soon swelled their number. French Huguenots organized a church at Charleston, South Carolina, in 1686. About 1720 a presbytery was organized in South Carolina from these groups, but it did not join the General Assembly until 1811.

1720

Francis Makemie. Francis Makemie is the real father of organized American Presbyterianism. Before his time, as we have just seen, Presbyterians were to be found scattered over the colonies in isolated congregations, but without having over them any presbytery, which is essential to the complete functioning of the Presbyterian system. To Makemie goes the credit of organizing the first presbytery, and of setting the infant church—now for the first time truly a corporate church—on its illustrious way.

Makemie the father of American Presbyterianism

Colonel William Stevens, a member of the Council of Maryland Province, wrote to the Presbytery of Laggan in Ireland in 1680, urging that ministers be sent across the sea to Maryland and Virginia. In response, the Irish presbytery ordained and sent a young Irishman, Francis Makemie, educated in Scotland, who was willing to obey the Macedonian call to America.

With unusual energy Makemie supported himself by private business enterprise and preached the gospel without remuneration. From the Carolinas to New York he nobly fulfilled his ministry. Population was scattered, distances were great, horses were scarce, and roads were either nonexistent or hopelessly poor. The traveler was continually in danger from Indians or more civilized robbers. In Maryland, settlements were usually along the rivers, and up these Makemie patiently made his way, bringing Christian exhortation and cheer to many a forgotten cabin. Perhaps as early as 1683 he organized Presbyterian churches at Rehoboth and Snow Hill, Maryland, and later several others near by.

The Presbytery. The work for which Francis Makemie will always be most gratefully remembered was his leadership in organizing the first enduring presbytery in America, correctly known as "the Presbytery," or "the General Presbytery." It was composed of seven ministers: three of these were from Ireland, one from Scotland, and three from New England. Unfortunately the first page of the minute book is lost, but it may be safely inferred that the first meeting of the Presbytery was held some time in 1706. The first recorded meeting was a special one at Freehold on December 27, 1706, to ordain a certain John Boyd.

Dec. 27, 1706

First presbytery meeting at Freehold.

The changed atmosphere after the English Toleration Act of 1689, as well as the altered circumstances of Presbyterians in the New World, caused many Presbyterians in the American colonies to favor religious toleration, and even religious liberty. Francis Makemie, the month after he attended the meeting of presbytery to ordain John Boyd, made an important contribution to the cause of religious toleration when he was arrested in New York for preaching without a license from the governor. After imprisonment for six weeks, he was acquitted, but was forced to pay the entire costs of the trial. The high-handed action of Governor Cornbury in these proceedings contributed to Cornbury's recall soon afterward. Makemie's victory for religious toleration was a notable one.

Religious toleration

As originally organized, the Presbytery included congregations only in Maryland, Delaware, and Philadelphia. Some of the Puritan Presbyterian churches of New Jersey and Long Island joined the Presbytery in the years immediately following, so that by 1716 it had grown from the original seven members to seventeen. The ministers from Philadelphia north to Long Island were mostly of New England origin; those in Delaware and Maryland, Scottish or Irish.

The only student for the ministry whom this Presbytery took under its care was David Evans, a Welshman, in 1710. He was ordained in 1714.

Though the Presbytery was gradually growing, its task was arduous. It covered a tremendous area in days when transportation was most difficult. The people were poor and widely scattered. Ministers were scarce, the most readily available places of training being the University of Edinburgh and Glasgow University in Scotland and the New England colleges, Harvard and Yale.

A few years after its organization, the Presbytery wrote to Presbyterians of London, Dublin, and Glasgow for financial aid. The plan seems to have been to persuade each of these centers to support a minister in America. "It pays to advertise," for by 1715 London and Scotland were feeling a new interest in the infant American Presbytery.

This Presbytery was not organized by any higher ecclesiastical body, nor under any political pressure or royal encouragement. It was a spontaneous growth, rising to fill a need clearly felt. In the years that followed, it became evident that Presbyterianism was the free preference of thousands scattered throughout the American colonies.

More Presbyterians Come. The years following the Restoration of the English monarchy in 1660 brought thousands of persecuted Presbyterians from Scotland and Ireland to America. The Test Act of 1713 in Ireland further increased the flow of emigration from that land. The Scotch-Irish newcomers settled most thickly in the middle colonies, especially in Pennsylvania. Great Britain's loss proved to be America's gain. The new Presbytery grew so fast that it appeared advisable to organize a General Synod, as we shall see in the next chapter.

CHAPTER VII

The General Synod

The Synod Organized. Numerically the Presbytery proved to be a great "success." Quite a number of the adjacent Presbyterian ministers and congregations soon saw fit to connect themselves with this much-needed organization. With seventeen ministers on its roll in 1716, the Presbytery transformed itself into a General Synod, having under it the four presbyteries of Long Island (comprising the churches of New York and New Jersey), Philadelphia (comprising the churches of Pennsylvania), New Castle (comprising the churches of Delaware), and Snow Hill (comprising the churches of Maryland). The Synod held its first meeting the next year, but the Presbytery of Snow Hill never came into being as planned.

At its first meeting in 1717 the Synod set apart a "fund for pious uses," with Jedediah Andrews, pastor in Philadelphia, as treasurer. The Synod of Glasgow contributed generously to this sum, and continued liberal financial aid to the infant church for many years.

The General Synod proved to have even more drawing power than the old Presbytery. Jonathan Dickinson, of Elizabethtown (modern Elizabeth), New Jersey, who was to prove himself one of the outstanding Presbyterians of the colonial period, and John Pierson, of Woodbridge, attended the first meeting of Synod. Two years later Joseph Webb was ordained by neighboring ministers to serve as pastor at Newark, and joined one of the presbyteries under the Synod. The new Presbytery of Long Island served as a rallying point for the Presbyterian churches of the Long Island region, though most of them did not at once join it.

The Adopting Act. At this time "rationalism" was leading some to try to express Christian truth in such a way that human reason could understand it more completely. As a result altered views of Christ's deity were being suggested by some. As a safeguard, British Presbyterians were considering requiring all ministers to "subscribe" the Westminster Confession of Faith, that is, to declare that it expressed their own beliefs. As the American churches were continually being supplied with ministers educated in Great Britain, the American Presbytery of New Castle requested the General Synod to require all ministers entering the church to subscribe the Westminster Confession. Strenuous opposition to the suggestion was raised by many in the Synod, including the distinguished Jonathan Dickinson. In general, the men of Scottish and Irish origin took the conservative position in favor of subscription to the Confession; and men of New England origin took the more liberal position of opposition to subscription. More than once in its later history the Presbyterian Church was to be vexed by this liberal-conservative division.

Liberal-Conservative division arises.

A split in the church was threatening when the situation was saved by approving the Adopting Act, drafted chiefly by Jonathan Dickinson. It provided that every entering minister, or candidate for the ministry, was to declare the Westminster Confession and the Larger and Shorter Catechisms to be "in all the essential and necessary articles, good forms of sound words and systems of Christian doctrine." If there were parts of these standards which any minister could not accept, he should state his scruples to his presbytery or to the Synod, and this body would decide whether the matter was "essential" enough to warrant his exclusion. The Adopting Act was passed by the Synod in 1729. Thus the exercise of intelligence and Christian good will saved the church from division, without the sacrifice of convictions by either party.

Compromise solution.

Presbyterian Life. Presbyterian church life in the period around 1730 was very different from what it is today. The Lord's Supper was celebrated twice a year, with appropriate sermons preached on the preceding Thursday, Friday, and Saturday. At the Communion service itself the atmosphere was one of deep solemnity. Long tables extended from the pulpit to the door. All those persons who had "tokens" might partake of the sacred feast.

Church members took their religion seriously. Upon arriving home, it was customary for them to discuss the sermon, and often to compare the preacher's doctrines, point for point, with Scripture. The minister's salary was often paid in kind: wheat, Indian corn, hemp, or linen yarn were often specified in his call.

Life was crude, but not illiterate, for the Scotch-Irish immigrants brought along schoolmasters. "It was rare to find one . . . who could not read and who did not possess a Bible." Parents presenting children for baptism were questioned as to their habits of family worship. The Shorter Catechism was a staple of spiritual diet, learned at home, recited at school, repeated to the minister. Congregations were divided into "quarters," with one elder particularly responsible for the spiritual welfare of each quarter. The people of a quarter were frequently collected—often in a kitchen or barn—to be catechized by the minister.

The Log College. Because of its Calvinistic emphasis on the Word of God, Presbyterianism has always stressed the necessity of a highly educated ministry to expound the Word. Quite soon, therefore, American Presbyterians became active in establishing means of educating candidates for the ministry. This was soon followed by active promotion of higher education in general.

At first ministers gave theological instruction in their own homes. A somewhat more ambitious venture was the so-called "Log College" conducted by William Tennent who was pastor at Neshaminy, Pennsylvania. In a little log house, about twenty feet square, Tennent instructed his four notable sons and other men who went forth to play a leading role in the ecclesiastical and educational life of the day. George Whitefield wrote in his *Journal,* "To me it seemed to resemble the school of the old prophets." About eighteen graduated from this institution. Presbyterians of today look back with real pride to this humble but truly great bit of pioneer Presbyterian education.

Though Tennent's "Log College" closed some years before his death in 1746, the influence of his work kept growing. Academies, similar to Tennent's school, were soon founded at Faggs Manor, Pequea, and West Nottingham. These, as well as later institutions inspired by such early precedents, graduated an amazingly high percentage of ecclesiastical and educational leaders.

The College of New Jersey was chartered in 1746, shortly after the closing of the "Log College." Though it was not officially a continuation of the "Log College," it did for some time perpetuate its spirit, four of its first twelve trustees being "Log College" men. After being briefly located in Elizabethtown and Newark, it moved in 1756 to Princeton and in 1896 became Princeton University. It has well been called a "mother of colleges," and, during the days of its predominatingly Presbyterian character, it constituted one more evidence of the effective interest Presbyterians have had in education since colonial days.

The Great Awakening. Church life in this period was serious, even to the point of severity, but we shall err greatly if we look back too wistfully to the "good old days." In 1733 the General Synod expressed concern over the decline of piety, and urged ministers to pay special attention to pastoral visitation and to the encouragement of family and private worship. The proportion of the population who were church members was far smaller than it is today. In Virginia not more than one person in twenty was a member of a church. Even in Puritan New England, the percentage of church members was appallingly low. Grandchildren of the devout Puritan and Scotch-Irish settlers were often utterly godless. Apprehensive preachers spoke of the menace of barbarism. But a better day for American Christianity was about to dawn.

In the 1720's, Jacob Frelinghuysen, pastor of the Dutch Reformed Church at Raritan, New Jersey, was insisting on the necessity of conversion and visible evidences of new spiritual life in professing Christians. His influence extended to a young Presbyterian pastor, Gilbert Tennent, son of William Tennent, founder of the famous Log College at Neshaminy, Pennsylvania. Gilbert Tennent, who was located at New Brunswick, New Jersey, a few miles from Frelinghuysen's parish, began, in 1728, with very evident success, to preach the necessity of conversion and new life. Jonathan Dickinson, at Elizabethtown, and many other ministers caught the revival spirit.

This "Great Awakening," as it is well called, was not confined to the middle colonies, or to any one denomination. In 1734, Jonathan Edwards, Congregational minister at Northampton, Massachusetts, began to preach with life-changing power. During the first year more than three hundred in his community professed conversion. Within six years the revival was quite general throughout New England. In a two-year period, between 25,000 and 50,000 members were added to the New England churches out of a total population of only about 300,000. At Enfield, Connecticut, Edwards preached so graphic a sermon on "Sinners in the Hands of an Angry God" that several times he had to pause for quiet, for all over the building men and women were crying aloud in their distress, feeling that they were slipping into hell.

George Whitefield, son of an English tavern keeper, graduate of Oxford, friend of the Wesleys, and greatest English preacher of his generation, made many trips from England to the American colonies between 1738 and 1770. He traveled from Georgia to New England, giving a unity to the Awakening which it had hitherto lacked. "Under the spell of his matchless oratory men wept, women fainted, and hundreds professed conversion."

In spite of its emotional excesses, which occasionally almost produced hysteria, the Great Awakening was a permanent blessing to America. Hitherto Christianity in the colonies had been a rather austere enterprise for the spiritually select; now the gospel came home to the common man with overpowering effectiveness. The Great Awakening decided that America should be, not a pagan, but a Christian land. It stimulated moral earnestness, missionary zeal, philanthropy, co-operation across denominational lines, and the founding of educational institutions. It gave new value and confidence to the average man and so contributed to the development of democracy in America. It strengthened the nonestablished churches more than the established, and so helped to prepare for religious freedom. But later revivalism's emphasis on emotion often undermined sober religious thinking, and its almost exclusive interest in individuals greatly weakened the idea of the church.

The Schism of 1741. One of the less happy by-products of the Great Awakening was the censorious spirit which it developed in some of its chief sponsors. Gilbert Tennent, leader of the revivalists, or "New Side" party, in the Presbytery of New Brunswick, which had been established by the Synod in 1738, was second to none in invective. In 1740, at Nottingham, Pennsylvania, he preached a scathing sermon on "The Danger of an Unconverted Ministry," filled with denunciations of his fellow ministers. Members of the Synod in 1741, after adopting a paper protesting against the spirit and practices of Tennent and his party, declared, in a quite irregular way, that the New Brunswick Presbytery was no longer a part of the Synod. In 1745 this Presbytery, together with the Presbyteries of New York and New Castle, formed the Synod of New York. Thus the church presented the sad spectacle of being divided into two entirely independent and even hostile bodies, the Synod of Philadelphia and the Synod of New York—the former known as the "Old Side" and the latter as the "New Side"—at the very moment when the full strength of a united church was needed for aggressive missionary work along the rapidly developing western frontier.

The Reunion of 1758. Not long after the division, friendly overtures between the two synods began to be exchanged. Reunion was achieved in 1758, with each side making concessions to the other. The Synod of Philadelphia consented to regard the offensive protest of 1741 as the act of the individual members who signed it, and not as the official act of the synod. The antirevival group also made the important concession that thereafter candidates for the ministry should be examined as to their "experimental acquaintance with religion." The revival group on its part agreed that irresponsible and unproved denunciations of fellow ministers were to be forbidden; that ministers might not intrude uninvited into the congregations of others; and that greater deference was to be paid to the authority of the church courts. By these and other provisions, the two synods were reunited in 1758 on the basis of the Westminster Standards under the new name of the Synod of New York and Philadelphia. Here, as on a similar occasion in 1869, the church, by reuniting on a platform of mutual concessions, tacitly acknowledged the futility and unwisdom of having divided.

Frontier Missions. Some of the noblest spirits modern Christianity has produced are to be found among the early American missionaries to the Indians. One of the most famous of these was David Brainerd, who labored among the Indians from Freehold, New Jersey, to the Susquehanna River. He died a discouraged man in 1747, after only four years of service, but the story of his life, published by Jonathan Edwards, stimulated countless readers to missionary endeavor.

White settlers on the western frontiers were also an object of missionary activity. In 1755 the Synod of New York organized the Presbytery of Hanover, extending from western Pennsylvania to Georgia. The eloquent Samuel Davies, later president of the College of New Jersey, had labored there years before the presbytery was erected. This frontier presbytery became a mother of presbyteries.

In 1781 the Synod of New York and Philadelphia organized the Presbytery of Redstone in western Pennsylvania. This was the far west of the day. Settlers dressed in deerskins, used blankets for overcoats, and lived in log cabins. Worship was held under the trees or in a fort, no church building having existed, so far as is known, before 1790. Often the men came armed, for fear of Indians, and stacked their guns before worshiping, while one of their number stood guard. Wayne's victory over the Indians in 1794 ended the danger. Though material comforts were lacking in these earliest days, many of the pioneers were highly educated men, with deep religious convictions. The ministers shared the hardships, sometimes traveling long distances through forest trails in their lonely and dangerous service. Often they must supplement their inadequate salaries by farming or teaching.

It was such a spirit that won the great American West for Jesus Christ. We are not surprised that soon the growing Presbyterian Church felt the need of organizing a General Assembly to direct its expanding work. But of this we shall hear in the next chapter.

CHAPTER VIII

The General Assembly Organized

The American Revolution. Presbyterians were second to none in their patriotic devotion to the cause of American independence. Religious as well as economic and political causes underlay the American Revolution. Many non-Anglicans, especially the Presbyterians, were alarmed at the desire of the English Church to send a resident bishop to the American colonies. Twice in the seventeenth and once in the eighteenth century, this plan had almost been carried into effect. In 1767, Dr. T. B. Chandler, an American Anglican, sought to show non-Anglicans that the coming of a bishop would be no threat to the religious liberties of other denominations. But the discussion that followed only revived the fears of dissenters. Presbyterians could not forget that many of their immediate ancestors had come to America to escape persecution from government-supported Anglican prelates in England, Scotland, and Ireland. They had no desire to see similar calamities overtake them in their new home, and were ready to resist with the sword if necessary. Most of the other dissenting bodies felt as the Presbyterians did. On the other hand, most Episcopalians outside of the South favored the "loyalist," or British side, in the Revolution against the "patriot," or American side.

Social Contract Theory from Presby. pulpits.

Leaders of the American Revolution used the social-contract theory to justify their revolt against the mother country. As we saw in Chapter V, English Puritans had helped to develop the social-contract theory of government which was like their own covenant theology. It was quite natural, therefore, for American Presbyterian ministers to make their pulpits ring with these ideas. Preachers, like secular patriots, repeatedly charged that George III by his "tyranny"

62

had broken his contract with his American subjects, and that therefore his subjects were released from their allegiance. This was an important contribution to the war effort, for Presbyterian influence in the colonies was great. New England, it is true, was predominantly Congregational, and in the southern colonies the Episcopal Church was established. But in the middle colonies an important proportion of the population was Presbyterian.

May 17, 1775, was a stirring day in the Presbyterian Synod of New York and Philadelphia, meeting in Philadelphia. In the preceding month the first blood of the Revolution had been shed at Lexington. Early in the same month the Second Continental Congress had assembled in Philadelphia. The whole city and country were seething with excitement. In the distraction of these feverish days only twenty-four ministers and five elders were present. The Synod appointed a day of "solemn fasting, humiliation, and prayer" for all the congregations. The Synod also drafted a pastoral letter, which wielded a strong, though restrained, influence for the patriot side.

Presbyterians individually were active in support of the cause of independence. The most distinguished minister of the Presbyterian Church, Dr. Witherspoon, was a member of the Continental Congress and a signer of the Declaration of Independence. Charles Thomson, secretary of the Continental Congress, was a Presbyterian elder. Joseph Clark and James F. Armstrong, later Moderators of the Presbyterian General Assembly, were both military officers in the war. Indeed, so universal was the patriotic ardor of the Presbyterian ministers that Dr. Inglis, Tory rector of Trinity Church, New York, wrote in 1776, "I do not know one Presbyterian minister, nor have I been able, after strict inquiry, to hear of any who did not by preaching and every effort in their power promote all the measures of the Continental Congress, however extravagant."

Religious Toleration After the Revolution. We today are inclined to think of complete religious freedom as being characteristic of America. But this did not become the case until after the Revolution. In 1774 nine of the colonies had churches "established," or specially favored, by law. The establishment of Congregationalism was not ended in Connecticut until 1818, and in Massachusetts not until 1833.

At the close of the Revolution, however, the separation of church and state in America became assured. With the support of the English Government removed by independence, the Episcopal Church sank into the position of an unofficial minority body. Outside of New England, no one denomination was sufficiently strong numerically to secure official recognition as the preferred, or established, church.

In view of the strength of Presbyterianism in the middle colonies, some suspected the Presbyterian Church of cherishing the ambition to become established. But, as we have seen, Presbyterians, amid changing thinking in the English-speaking world, and amid the special conditions of colonial life, had before this become hearty converts to the ideal of religious liberty. Therefore the Synod of New York and Philadelphia renounced any such intention by adopting the following minute in 1781: "The Synod do solemnly and publicly declare that they ever have, and still do, renounce and abhor the principles of intolerance, and we do believe that every peaceable member of civil society ought to be protected in the full and free exercise of their religion." This splendid declaration voices the best of Presbyterian and of American conviction on the subject of religious freedom.

Organization of the General Assembly. With the winning of the Revolution and the securing of independence, the spirit of patriotic nationalism swept the United States. Most of the churches, catching this spirit, organized themselves on a national basis at this time. The former Anglicans now formed themselves into the Protestant Episcopal Church of the United States of America. Their securing of American bishops was viewed by Presbyterians and others with good will, for the former opposition to bishops had been due, not to a fear of bishops as such, but to a fear of bishops supported by government authority and power. The Dutch Reformed, German Reformed, and Methodist Churches all formed national organizations in this period. The Congregationalists began to form state organizations; and the Roman Catholics laid the foundation for their national organization by the consecration of a bishop of Baltimore.

In 1785 the Presbyterian Synod of New York and Philadelphia, also responsive to the new spirit of nationalism, felt that a more adequate national organization for the church would be a General Assembly, constituted of elected delegates and containing synods subordinate to it, rather than the existing Synod, composed of all the ministers of the church and an elder from every congregation. Accordingly, the Synod in 1788 organized a General Assembly, with the four subordinate synods of New York and New Jersey, Philadelphia, Virginia, and the Carolinas, including a total of sixteen presbyteries, 177 ministers, 111 probationers, and 419 churches.

[margin note: 1788 General Assembly Organized]

The Synod of 1788 amended the Westminster Confession of Faith and the Larger Catechism to be agreeable to the new American theory of the separation of church and state. The Westminster Directory for the Worship of God was so amended as to become almost a new work. These, together with the Shorter Catechism and a Form of Government and Discipline, the latter of which was specially prepared for the occasion, were to be the standards of the reorganized church. It was further provided that these standards could be amended only with the approval of the presbyteries. As one of the conditions of ordination, ministers were required to answer affirmatively the following question: "Do you sincerely receive and adopt the Confession of Faith of this church, as containing the system of doctrine taught in the Holy Scriptures?" This is still the formula of creedal subscription for ministers, elders, and deacons.

The first General Assembly met in the Second Presbyterian Church of Philadelphia in May, 1789, with John Witherspoon as its presiding officer. At the very moment when this first Assembly was meeting in Philadelphia, the first United States Congress under the new Constitution was meeting in New York. The Assembly appointed a committee, with John Witherspoon as chairman, to draft an address to President George Washington.

[margin note: 1789 Phila. first meeting]

Claims have sometimes been made that the United States Constitution was deliberately patterned after the Presbyterian form of government. It is nearer the truth to say that resemblances existing between the two are due to the fact that the principles of representative government upon which both rest were the common heritage of the men and women of the Revolutionary period, two thirds of whom came of Calvinistic stock, and most of whom had been influenced by the political thought of the Puritan Revolution.

[margin note: Federal & U-S. Cons Presby. Constitutions drew from same sources available to all.]

It is, however, no exaggeration to say that our sister churches in America have been greatly influenced by some of the fundamental principles of Presbyterian polity, such as the equality of the clergy and the representation of laymen in the governing bodies of the church.

Spiritual Decline. The American Revolution, like most wars, was followed by a period of alarming moral and spiritual decline throughout the land. Countless ministers and laymen had abandoned parish duties for military service. The buildings of the Presbyterians, who were conspicuous in their devotion to the patriot cause, were often used by the enemy as barracks or stables or destroyed by the fortunes of war. America's alliance with France had opened the door to the influence of Voltaire and Rousseau, and other forms of French infidelity and radical social views. Tom Paine's *Age of Reason* made antireligious "freethinking" popular with many. The Presbyterian General Assembly of 1798 declared, "We perceive with pain and fearful apprehension a general dereliction of religious principles and practice among our fellow citizens . . . and an abounding infidelity, which in many instances tends to atheism itself." But, once more, showers of blessing were very near.

Another Revival. In 1798-1801 there occurred a revival which soon became almost nation-wide. Nowhere were its manifestations more striking than in Kentucky, which in those early days was a typically lawless frontier. Speculation, danger, hard labor, low physical gratifications, quarreling, and fighting were the elements of daily life.

In 1799, Rev. James McGready persuaded a few members from one of his churches in Logan County, Kentucky, to pray an hour a week and one day a month for the conversion of unbelievers. Within a few months a woman was converted who by zeal in personal work soon won nine or ten others. During the next two years the revival spread to other parishes, now being accompanied by strange physical effects: those under conviction of sin would groan, cry out, or sprawl on the floor.

By 1800 the movement had become widespread in Kentucky, and "camp meetings" appeared for the first time in America in connection with this revival. These were real camps. Some slept in tents, others in covered wagons, arranged around a hollow square, where the religious meetings were held. A platform of logs was the pulpit; rows of logs were the seats for the audience. A spectator in 1801 says of a Kentucky camp-meeting revival: "At one time I saw at least five hundred swept down in a moment, as if a battery of a thousand guns had been opened upon them; and then immediately followed shrieks and shouts that rent the very heavens. My hair rose upon my head, my whole frame trembled, the blood ran cold in my veins, and I fled for the woods." One historian reminds us that these camp meetings must have been impressive at night. The campfires gleamed, while candles and lanterns hanging from the trees illuminated branches and faces with a dancing glow. To this were added fervent prayers, the chant of the hymns, and enthusiastic exhortations—punctuated by sobs, shrieks, and cries for mercy. Those who came to scoff frequently remained to weep.

This revival, which was not localized in Kentucky but, as we have said, was quite general throughout the nation, overthrew the "free thought" and infidelity that had followed the revolution. Sunday schools now first became widespread in the United States. Home missions, foreign missions, and ministerial education developed greatly in the decades following the revival.

The Cumberland Presbyterian Church originated at this time. The Transylvania Presbytery and the Cumberland Presbytery, which grew out of it, ordained men whose education was unsatisfactory, and who frankly rejected part of the Westminster Confession of Faith as teaching "fatalism." As a result of the action of the Presbyterian Synod of Kentucky and of the General Assembly, a majority of the Cumberland Presbytery, in 1810, created an entirely separate denomination, later known as the Cumberland Presbyterian Church. A happy event of the twentieth century was the reunion in 1906 by organic merger of the Presbyterian Church in the United States of America and the Cumberland Presbyterian Church, by that time grown to be a large and influential denomination.

Missions and Expansion. It is in no way derogatory to sister denominations to say that in 1800 the Presbyterian Church was the most influential single denomination in the country. It had a learned ministry; a sizable membership that was distributed, though not uniformly, over the country as a whole; an efficient central government supplied by the new General Assembly; prestige from its unquestioned patriotism; and—together with many of the other churches—renewed spiritual vigor from the recent revival. The church was growing rapidly. By 1800 there were twenty-six presbyteries, as compared with sixteen some ten years before. In 1789, the year of the first Assembly, there had been 419 churches, as compared with 511 in 1803.

The greatest task facing the church for many years to come was the evangelization of the frontier. The new General Assembly soon directed all congregations to make annual collections for home missions and to forward them to the Assembly. The church was determined to try to do its part to win America for Christ.

CHAPTER IX

The Plan of Union

The Plan of Union Adopted. By the opening of the nineteenth century there was becoming visible a distinctly "American" type of Christianity. It had a common heritage from English Puritanism and had been further shaped by common American experiences like frontier life and revivalism. It included such groups as Presbyterians, Congregationalists, Baptists, and, in part, Low Church Episcopalians. The closely related Dutch and German Reformed had kinship with these bodies. Revivalistically inclined newer movements, like the Methodists and Disciples, also had much in common with them. Presently some Lutherans, though heirs of a different form of the Protestant heritage, were being drawn toward the emerging type.

A new American patriotism was greatly strengthening the forces of heritage and religious environment that were working for Christian unity at this time. Together Americans had won the war for independence. The Federal Constitution had further strengthened national unity, which was increased later by the War of 1812. Thus the stage was set for greater Christian co-operation than Americans had yet attempted, a kind of forerunner of the modern ecumenical movement.

Co-operation between Presbyterians and Congregationalists came with particular readiness and formed the nucleus of the growing unity. Relations between these two bodies had been cordial during the colonial period and since. Both accepted the Reformed or Calvinistic doctrines and both used a simple Puritan type of worship. The chief differences were in church government, the Congregationalists having no presbyteries over the local congregations. But even

at this point the Congregationalists, with a central General Association in each New England state, seemed to be coming somewhat
nearer to the Presbyterian practice.

The great revival of 1798-1801 inspired the Presbyterians to send
missionaries into the frontiers of central and western New York,
where they met missionaries sent by the New England Congregationalists. Would the two churches set up rival organizations in the
needy field, or could some method be found of eliminating competi-
tion? With a view to solving this problem, Jonathan Edwards, the
younger, when a Presbyterian delegate to the General Association of
Connecticut in 1800, suggested a "Plan of Union." The next year the
Plan was adopted by both the General Association and the General
Assembly.

The Plan of Union was an ingenious arrangement making it possible for congregations to be connected with both the Congregational
and the Presbyterian denominations at the same time, and to be
served by pastors of either. Presbyterian churches might be represented in the Congregational associations by their elders, while Congregational churches could be represented in the presbyteries by com-
mitteemen. Disputed cases might be referred either to presbytery or
to a special council. The Plan worked so well that in 1808 the Middle
Association of Congregationalists in New York State accepted an
invitation to become an integral part of the Presbyterian Synod of
Albany, without ceasing to be Congregationalists. The Congregationalists, on their part, were so well satisfied with the Plan that for many
years they formed no separate organization of ministers in New York
State west of the Military Tract.

But, as we shall see, the Plan eventually proved impracticable, being by many derisively dubbed "Presbygational." To have formed an
entirely new denomination with a new form of church government
that was a cross between Presbyterianism and Congregationalism
might have proved feasible. But to have a large group of churches
belonging at the same time to two denominations that were distinct
and, in important respects, dissimilar, opened the way for difficulties.

The "Benevolent Empire." Even more important than the Plan of
Union as an example of the growing spirit of Christian unity in this

early national period was the so-called "Benevolent Empire," or system of voluntary societies, closely resembling similar societies organized by Dissenters in England a little earlier. In keeping with the individualistic spirit of revivalism, these societies were conducted by Christian individuals, not by church bodies. They were, therefore, "nondenominational" rather than "interdenominational."

Some of the societies devoted themselves to missionary and other religious activities; while others, organized on the same pattern and with strong Christian motivation, crusaded for moral reform— against such evils as slavery, intemperance, and war. These societies formed a kind of network, often with interlocking directorates, reaching over a large part of the country, and drawing support from individuals in many denominations, but with their principal strength in the Northeast, and with their principal leadership supplied by Congregationalists, with Presbyterians second. The influence of this "Benevolent Empire" on religious and social life was very great.

Foreign Missions. The first of these national voluntary societies to be organized was the American Board of Commissioners for Foreign Missions, formed in 1810.

In 1806, Samuel J. Mills, who had been fired with foreign missionary zeal by his Congregational pastor in Newport, Rhode Island, entered Williams College. With young Mills as their inspiration, a group of students of the college gathered near a lonely haystack and solemnly pledged themselves to missionary service. Later most of them entered Andover Seminary, where they were joined by others like-minded. In 1810 some of the men of this group asked the Congregational General Association of Massachusetts to begin foreign missionary activity, and offered themselves as missionaries. The General Association rose to the occasion, and at that very meeting organized the American Board of Commissioners for Foreign Missions, commonly known as the American Board. In February, 1812, Judson, Rice, Newell, Nott, and Hall, with their wives, sailed for India in two parties as the first American missionaries to a foreign land. By 1879 the influence, direct and indirect, of the little "haystack meeting" had resulted in the formation of at least five separate foreign missionary boards in America.

In 1811 the American Board invited the Presbyterian General Assembly of the following year to form a similar board of its own to co-operate with them. The Assembly declined, deciding instead to commend the work of the American Board to Presbyterians for their support. The Congregationalists responded to this reply in the same generous spirit in which it had been made, and added a number of Presbyterian ministers and laymen to membership on the American Board.

In 1817, the Presbyterian, Dutch Reformed, and Associate Reformed Churches organized the United Foreign Missionary Society, which had as its avowed purpose "to spread the gospel among the Indians of North America, the inhabitants of Mexico and South America, and in other portions of the heathen and anti-Christian world." In 1826 this society, observing with satisfaction the splendid foreign missionary work being done by the American Board, voted to transfer all its work and property to that Board. Until the formation of the Presbyterian Board of Foreign Missions in 1837, a majority of Presbyterians continued to aid in supporting the work of the American Board.

Home Missions. Geography determined that the most important responsibility of Christianity in America was to be that of winning the West for Christ. The nineteenth century was the period when this gigantic task was in large part performed.

The year 1808, with its depression caused by Jefferson's embargo policy, enacted the previous year, drove thousands to seek better fortune on the western frontier. Two hundred and thirty-six west-bound wagons were counted passing through a village near Pittsburgh in a single day. Western New York witnessed similar sights. Villages sprang up in the West almost overnight. In the single year 1811 General Harrison's victory over the Indians at Tippecanoe, the beginning of the construction of the Cumberland Road, and the launching of the first Mississippi steamboat all further encouraged western migration. The Erie Canal, begun in 1816 and completed in 1825, made western New York more accessible. The trek westward was so rapid that by 1829 nine of the eleven new states were west of the Alleghenies, containing more than a third of the population of the entire country. Would the Christian churches be able to rise to the emergency?

None of the churches was better prepared for the task than the Presbyterian. The Scotch-Irish—enthusiastic Presbyterians by tradition—were the latest wave of immigrants. Scattered along the frontier from New England to the Carolinas, they would be particularly amenable to Presbyterian appeals. In 1802 the Presbyterian General Assembly erected a "Standing Committee of Missions," consisting of four ministers and three elders. Three years later it was found too small for its great task and was enlarged. Among their other duties the members of this committee were "to collect, during the recess of the Assembly, all the information in their power relative to the concerns of missions and missionaries," and to submit their findings at each meeting of the General Assembly. This missions committee proved itself a timely aid. Almost at once fervent appeals for help came from northern, central, and western New York, then from Ohio, Indiana, Kentucky, and Tennessee. By 1811 the work had expanded so much that the Assembly was forced to appeal to the churches for increased aid. The preceding year the Assembly had been able to report that in western New York the number of ministers had increased from two to almost fifty in eleven years. In 1816 the Standing Committee's name was changed to the "Board of Missions," and it was given greater independence of action though it was still fully subject to the General Assembly.

The spirit of Christian co-operation, so characteristic of this period, found further expression in 1826 in the formation of another of the voluntary societies, namely, the American Home Missionary Society. At first largely Presbyterian in membership, it was soon greatly augmented by the Congregationalists, and proved itself an important agent in organizing and developing new churches under the Presbyterian-Congregational Plan of Union of 1801. The American Home Missionary Society was the first such home missionary organization operating on a national and nondenominational basis, and aided weak churches all over the country. By 1835 this society had 719 agents and missionaries.

But the work was only fairly begun during this period. Samuel J. Mills, of haystack-meeting fame, who had been prevented by ill health from serving on the foreign mission field, investigated mission needs on the western and southwestern American frontier during the years 1812 and 1813. He reported that Ohio, with a population of 330,000, had only forty-nine Presbyterian and Congregational ministers; Indiana Territory, with a population of 25,000, had only one Presbyterian church and minister; and Illinois Territory, with a population of 13,000, had no Presbyterian church or minister at all. Much work still remained to be done.

All honor to these too easily forgotten pioneer missionaries, who labored so faithfully! Over lonely prairie and through virgin forest they rode their circuits, sleeping in rude shanties or beside open campfires. Impurity, gambling, drunkenness were among the evils that they encountered, and their most earnest efforts were frequently greeted with nothing but indifference or open hostility. Their remuneration was pathetically small—sometimes thirty-three dollars a month, sometimes a dollar a day. Later forty dollars a month was allowed, but not always accepted! One report, for example, tells us that a certain Mr. Chapman "received forty-five dollars and thirty-two cents, traveled two thousand miles, and preached above one hundred sermons." Another record states that James Hall, a missionary to Mississippi Territory, "served on his mission seven months and thirteen days, and received eighty-six dollars." It was the labors of such devoted men as these, in the Presbyterian and other churches, which decided that America, throughout its bounds, was to be a Christian land.

Other Nondenominational Agencies. The foreign and home missionary societies just mentioned did not exhaust the spirit of cooperation in religious work. Between 1812 and 1815 Samuel J. Mills made two tours of the West, covering almost 10,000 miles. In Kaskaskia, the capital of Illinois Territory, he had found only five Bibles in a hundred families. In older sections of the country as well there was often an amazing dearth of Bibles. As a result of such conditions, the American Bible Society was organized in 1816. In 1829 and 1830 this national Bible organization sought to place a Bible in every home in the land. Bibles were also given to immigrants as they entered the country.

In 1824 the American Sunday School Union was organized by men of various denominations. Fifteen years later the Union resolved to establish a Sunday school in every western community which had none. Much money was raised, enabling agents and missionaries to carry on their good work throughout the land. In 1825 the American Tract Society was founded.

The General Assembly of 1817, in a pastoral letter, showed its sympathy with the prevailing spirit of co-operation: "We are persuaded that all those periods and churches which have been favored with special revivals of religion have been also distinguished by visible union and concert in prayer. We entreat you, brethren, to cherish this union and concert."

Theological Seminaries. The rapidly expanding work of the church created a serious shortage of ministers, but the Presbyterian Church did not yield to the temptation to relax its traditionally high standards of ministerial education. To meet the problem, the General Assembly of 1809 asked the presbyteries which of three possibilities they preferred: (1) one strong seminary in a central location; (2) one seminary for the North and one for the South; (3) one seminary in each synod. The presbyteries favored the first suggestion, and the Assembly organized a seminary at Princeton, New Jersey, which opened with three students in August, 1812. Dr. Archibald Alexander and Dr. Samuel Miller were the first professors, with Dr. Charles Hodge added to the faculty a few years later.

Other Presbyterian seminaries were founded in this same period: 1818, Auburn; 1824, Union (in Virginia); 1827, Western; 1828, Columbia; 1829, Lane; 1830, McCormick; 1836, Union (in New York). Thus the Presbyterian Church was assured of a more adequate supply of properly trained ministers for its rapidly growing work.

CHAPTER X

The Church Divided

A New Period. Starting about 1830, American life entered a new phase. The spirit of nationalism, awakened by the Revolution and fostered by the War of 1812, began to give way to a spirit of bitter sectionalism, as the agricultural and slaveholding South and the industrial and "free" North became more and more sharply arrayed against each other. The rise to the Presidency of Andrew Jackson, with his new spirit of democracy, brought the "common man" into new power and prominence. Emotional instability and unbounded optimism characterized the new democratic spirit.

In the religious sphere, a third, or "Modern," period of American Christianity has been dated from about 1830, following, respectively, the "Puritan" period and the "Revivalist" period of the Great Awakening. In this modern period some groups reacted against the individualism of the emerging "American" type of Christianity (see Chapter IX), and, following similar churchly tendencies in Europe, emphasized the church as our spiritual mother and as necessary for the truest fellowship with Christ and with fellow Christians. Unfortunately, those who emphasized the church usually meant their own denomination, as there was no visible common church to which they could give their allegiance. The result was a regrettable tendency to pull out from the nondenominational voluntary societies.

This new denominational emphasis resembled in some ways the political shift from nationalism to sectionalism. The emotional instability of the new democracy had a religious parallel in the rise of many strange cults and sects in this period. But after a few decades the true churchly character of this modern religious period asserted itself more effectively, and divisiveness and emotionalism were replaced by a more historical and scientific and social spirit.

The Presbyterian Church Divides. In 1837 the Presbyterian Church was still the most influential religious body in America. In the thirty years between 1800 and 1830 it had increased from 20,000 to over 173,000 members, a growth proportionately more rapid than that of the country itself.

But for some years before 1837 there had been ominous rumblings of controversy between "Old School" and "New School" parties within the church on questions of church government and doctrine. The Old School, reflecting its "churchly" traditions and interest, was dissatisfied with the Plan of Union of 1801 with the Congregationalists, charging that the churches erected under the Plan were not truly Presbyterian at all, and that adequate control and discipline of them by the church courts was impossible. The Old School also felt that the Presbyterian Church should have its own denominational church boards, responsible to the General Assembly, rather than work through such nondenominational agencies as the American Board and the American Home Missionary Society. On the other hand, the New School, many members of which were of Congregational background and training, were quite satisfied with the Plan of Union and the nondenominational voluntary societies. They could point with pride to the fact that the Synod of Genesee in New York State and the two synods adjacent to it, all owing a large part of their growth to the Plan of Union, contained more communicant members in 1830 than the whole church had had in 1800.

The Old School and the New School also disagreed on certain matters of doctrine. Jonathan Edwards, one of the leaders of the Great Awakening in the eighteenth century, had restated—his followers said "improved"—some of the doctrines of Calvinism. Samuel Hopkins carried these innovations farther, and Nathaniel W. Taylor farther yet. "Hopkinsianism" and "Taylorism" were types of doctrine popular in the New School party.

In 1835 some members of the Old School party, becoming alarmed, circulated through the church an "Act and Testimony" over their signatures, warning of "the prevalence of unsound doctrine and laxity in discipline." Finding themselves in a majority in the General Assembly of 1837, the Old School men felt that the time for drastic action had arrived. They voted to abrogate the Plan of Union of 1801. They then took action stating that this abrogation was retroactive, and that the four Synods of Western Reserve, Utica, Geneva, and Genesee, organized under the Plan of Union, were no longer a part of the church. This definitely removed the New School party from the church.

The next year the commissioners from the exscinded presbyteries presented their credentials, but were refused seats. They organized themselves as a General Assembly and adjourned to another building. Thus the Presbyterian Church presented the strange spectacle of being divided into two almost equal denominations, having the same official name, the same doctrinal standards, the same form of government and worship, and covering about the same territory, yet completely separate and at times even hostile. The two churches during the years of division, 1837 to 1869, are popularly known as Old School and New School. The Old School contained about five ninths of the original membership, and was declared by the civil courts to be the legal successor of the undivided church. This tragic division occurred at the very time when the vast territorial expansion of the nation was about to challenge the church's utmost power.

Presbyterian Board of Foreign Missions. Before this division of 1837—that is, in the year 1831—the Synod of Pittsburgh, feeling the desirability of a foreign missionary enterprise under definitely denominational control, organized the Western Foreign Missionary Society. After the division of the church in 1837 the Old School Assembly created the Presbyterian Board of Foreign Missions to take over the funds and missions of the Western Foreign Missionary Society.

National Expansion. The period before us, 1837 to 1869, was the era of greatest geographical expansion in American history.

"Oregon," which then extended along the Pacific from modern California to Alaska, was claimed in its entirety by both Great Britain and the United States. By a treaty in 1818, renewed in 1827, the two nations agreed temporarily to occupy the region together. In 1835, Dr. Marcus Whitman, a physician of New York, went to Oregon under the American Board. "The [Presbyterian] Church on the Pacific Coast began with the mission work of Marcus Whitman, M.D., in Oregon, and by the organization of the church at Wai-ye-lat-poo (Kamiah) in 1838." In 1846 Great Britain and the United States, by treaty, agreed to divide Oregon between them, with 49° latitude as the boundary. A great territory was thus permanently acquired by the United States. The Treaty of Guadalupe Hidalgo, which ended the Mexican War in 1848, added to the United States an area from which at various times were carved the states of California, Nevada, Utah, Arizona, New Mexico, Texas, and parts of Wyoming, Colorado, and Oklahoma. This brought the United States practically to its present size.

In 1848 gold was discovered in California, and in 1858, and the years immediately following, gold, silver, copper, and lead were found in the Rocky Mountains at various points from Montana to Arizona. Mining prospectors and merchants flocked to the regions. The Homestead Act of 1862, whereby the government granted a hundred and sixty acres of free land to settlers upon certain conditions, served to develop rapidly the fertile lands between the older Middle West and the Rocky Mountain mining camps. In 1869 the first coast-to-coast railroad train completed its run. Thus a whole new country, larger than the original thirteen colonies, was rapidly being settled.

Immigration in this period and a continuing high birth rate were rapidly increasing the population of the whole nation. The census of 1790 had showed less than 4,000,000 people in the United States; that of 1850 revealed over 23,000,000, of whom more than 10,000,000 lived in the Mississippi basin. Between 1840 and 1869, 5,500,000 immigrants entered America, an increasing proportion of whom were Irish and German Catholics. Many began to talk of the dangers of a Catholic West.

The Presbyterian and other Protestant churches were meeting the challenge. It is estimated that between them they sometimes built a thousand churches a year in the Mississippi valley between 1850 and 1860. The achievement of building churches, Christian colleges, and schools; of organizing congregations and installing pastors in these new areas—in a word, the laying of Christian foundations for an entirely new country—all done in a comparatively short time, and supported by purely voluntary contributions, is one of the wonders of Christian history. The dates of erection of some of the Presbyterian synods of the West show that, during this and the following periods, Presbyterians were far from idle in the great task of Christian empire-building.

The Revival of 1857-1858. The year 1857 was a time of great depression, following prosperity unprecedented in America. Economic decline brought a spontaneous return to religious interests throughout the nation. In 1857 the doors of the consistory building of the Old Dutch Church in New York City were opened for prayer from noon to 1 P.M. Few responded at first, but before long the crowd overflowed into a second and a third room. By the spring of 1858 at least twenty such daily meetings were being held in New York City. Similar signs of deepened religious interest were witnessed throughout the country. No human leaders stood out in this revival as in the Great Awakening; instead, the effects were rather the result of spontaneous religious yearning on the part of the people themselves. The Young Men's Christian Association, a new and rapidly growing organization, fostered the work, and the secular press gave generous publicity. It is estimated that a million members were added to the American churches, of whom the Presbyterians received their proportionate share.

Presbyterian Colleges. The rapid western expansion of the nation, and with it of the church, created a great shortage of ministers on the frontier. But the Presbyterian Church refused to lower its high standards of ministerial education even in the face of the emergency. The result was that Presbyterianism in the new area grew in numbers less rapidly than might otherwise have been the case, but its educational influence was greatly enhanced.

Where there was no schoolmaster in a community, the Presbyterian minister would frequently teach a school of his own, in addition to his parish duties. As a result of this type of activity, of the forty colleges founded in the United States between 1780 and 1829, thirteen were established by Presbyterians and one by Presbyterians in conjunction with Congregationalists.

By the time of the outbreak of the Civil War, Presbyterians had founded forty-nine colleges and universities, located in twenty-one of the then thirty-four states of the Union. This was no small achievement for a single church, placing the Presbyterians before the Civil War in first place among the churches as an educational influence.

Presbyterians and Slavery. From 1830 to 1860 the all-absorbing political question in the nation was that of slavery. Most of the churches, by their official utterances, became, to a greater or less degree, involved in the problem. The Presbyterian Church, true to its Scotch-Irish conservatism, was cautious in its handling of the issue.

The first official utterance of the church came from the Synod of New York and Philadelphia in 1787: "They [the Synod] recommend it to all their people to use the most prudent measures, consistent with the interest and state of civil society, in the counties where they live, to procure eventually the final abolition of slavery in America." This action was reaffirmed by five General Assemblies.

In 1818 the General Assembly adopted an unusually strong utterance: "We consider the voluntary enslaving of one part of the human race by another . . . utterly inconsistent with the law of God . . . and . . . totally irreconcilable with the spirit and principles of the gospel of Christ."

After 1832 the discussion of slavery had become so embittered in the nation as a whole that the General Assembly of 1836 voted: "Resolved that this whole subject be indefinitely postponed."

After the division of 1837, the New School Church, with more than seven eighths of its membership in the North, took a more pronounced stand against slavery; while the Old School Church, with over one third of its membership in the South, maintained a more conservative attitude. As a result, the relatively small Southern section of the New School Church withdrew in 1857 to form the "United Synod of the Presbyterian Church." In the Old School Church, on the other hand, men of North and South continued in fellowship until the outbreak of the Civil War in 1861.

The Southern Church Organized. On April 12, 1861, Confederate forces bombarded the Federal Fort Sumter in Charleston harbor. Northern opinion was rapidly rallying behind the Federal Government; Southern opinion was preparing to support the Confederate Government.

In such a tense atmosphere, less than five weeks after the bombardment of Fort Sumter, the Old School General Assembly met in Philadelphia. As the Southern Presbyterians were still a part of the church, many in the Assembly hoped that a political declaration might be avoided. On the third day of the session, Dr. Gardiner Spring, of New York City, moved that a committee be appointed "to inquire into the expediency of making some expression of their devotion to the Union of these States." The motion was tabled. Most of the other denominations had lost their national unity, and the Old School Church was anxious to avoid the same fate.

Some days later Dr. Spring again took the initiative, offering resolutions committing the church to the Federal cause. By this time the whole country through the press was taking an interest in the deliberations of the Assembly. Would this influential church lend its moral support to the Union sentiment, rapidly crystallizing in the North, or not? Commissioners in the Assembly were continually receiving telegrams advising them how to vote. In such an atmosphere, and under such pressure of public opinion, the "Spring Resolutions" were adopted after five days of debate.

During the following months the Southern presbyteries of the Old School Church denounced this action of the Assembly, and withdrew from the church to organize the "Presbyterian Church in the Confederate States of America," which held its first meeting in Augusta, Georgia, on December 4, 1861. In 1864 this church merged with the United Synod of the Presbyterian Church, which was the Southern separation from the New School Church, thus reuniting Old School and New School in the South, though they were not yet reunited in the North. In 1865, the war being over, this merged Southern church changed its name to the "Presbyterian Church in the United States." In 1869 part of the Old School Synod of Kentucky, and in 1874 part of the Old School Synod of Missouri, joined the Southern church. The church today occupies a distinguished place among the Presbyterian churches of the world, notable for its urban strength and evangelical fervor.

The Civil War. During the Civil War, the various churches, both North and South, strained every effort to minister to the spiritual needs of the soldiers. The emergency very definitely fostered an inter-denominational spirit in both sections of the country, for Christian workers in the armies could not limit their ministrations to fellow sectarians.

In 1861 the Christian Commission was organized in New York, to send preachers, nurses, libraries, religious literature, and comforts to the men at the front. Its work was conducted by "delegates," or volunteer workers, drawn mostly from the churches. Many ministers served in this way for short periods. During the four years of the war, the Commission received more than $2,500,000, contributed largely through the churches.

The American Bible Society too was very active, giving Bibles and Testaments to both Union and Confederate armies. In 1864 the Society distributed almost a million copies, more than half of which went to the Union army and navy. The Tract Societies circulated thousands of tracts among the soldiers.

Many soldiers first entered the Christian life while in military service. Thus a great religious revival occurred in the Confederate army in 1863-1864. But the effects of war on the great majority of participants on both sides were, as always, demoralizing and brutalizing.

The period of reconstruction is an era that few in any section of the country recall today with any satisfaction. A particularly regrettable feature of it, from an ecclesiastical point of view, was the practice of Union armies as they advanced into the South of turning over to the use of Northern denominations and preachers of Northern sympathies the churches which they had taken. At the close of the war, the Northern Presbyterian Church tried, with notable lack of success, to set up churches, presbyteries, and synods composed of persons in the South who would repudiate slavery and support the Federal Government. These discourtesies to Southern feeling were very unfortunate.

The effects of the Civil War, as of any war, on the moral and spiritual life of the country were injurious. The interest of the churches was, for the time, sadly diverted. In the light of these facts, the era of corruption that overwhelmed the national Government need be considered no surprise. With the unhappy period of sectional strife and heightened denominational divisiveness at an end, we shall enter, in the following chapters, into a new era of interdenominational good will and expansiveness of spirit and sympathy.

CHAPTER XI

The Church Reunited

The Reunion. The Civil War was a watershed in American history. The closer unity that it forced upon all the states emphasized and strengthened forces already moving toward closer unity in political government, in business organization, and in church life. After the Civil War the West was being settled faster than ever, and Presbyterians realized that they could carry the gospel to the new settlers more effectively if their "Old School" and "New School" Churches were to unite. Reunion was aided by the fact that New School Presbyterians had developed a stronger sense of the church than they had previously had, and now conducted their missionary work by denominational "committees" similar to the Old School's "boards," rather than through the nondenominational voluntary societies. Then, too, theological change was in the air, and Old School Presbyterians were now less inclined to insist on the theological points that distinguished them from the New School. The result was that in 1869, after five years of negotiation, the Old School and New School Presbyterian Churches reunited on the basis of the Westminster Standards "pure and simple." The name of the reunited church was the Presbyterian Church in the United States of America—the name before the division and the name that each of the branches held during the division. The reunion of 1869, like the earlier reunion of 1758, underlined the futility and wastefulness of ever having divided.

Problems of Faith. The decades after the Civil War saw great changes in culture and thinking which created disturbing theological problems for the churches. In 1859, Charles Darwin had published

1869

85

his *Origin of Species*. Presbyterians, like other Christians, differed among themselves as to the relation between evolution and the Genesis story of creation, and as to how far ideas of development were to be applied to Christianity.

In the field of Biblical studies, scholars abroad, especially in Germany, using methods called "higher criticism," had been applying to the Bible the same scholarly analysis that had been applied to other literary and historical writings. They concluded that the Bible contained incorrect statements about history and science and other matters, and that traditional views concerning the authors and dates of Bible books were in many cases erroneous. Prof. Charles A. Briggs, of Union Seminary, New York, considered it crucially important that the new conclusions be accepted and interpreted by evangelical Christians and not become a monopoly of the enemies of historic Christianity. Therefore by articles in the 1880's and especially by an address in 1891 he introduced into the Presbyterian Church animated discussion of the new views.

Dr. Briggs believed deeply that God had revealed himself in the Old and New Testaments and especially in his Son, Jesus Christ, and that the Bible was a sufficiently trustworthy record of this revelation. But the vast majority of Presbyterians at that time believed that a more literal view of the Bible was necessary as a means of defending and expounding the Christian faith. Therefore the General Assembly in 1892 and 1893 declared that the original manuscripts of the Bible were "without error," and in 1893 suspended Dr. Briggs from the Presbyterian ministry. Time has sided with Dr. Briggs, until today, in a spirit of true Christian faith and reverence, similar views of the Bible are taught in Presbyterian seminaries and held by a large number of Presbyterian ministers.

In the latter part of the nineteenth century, Christians throughout the world were laying increased emphasis on God's love. Many Calvinists were turning away from some of the older interpretations of predestination. This explains the fact that the General Assembly of 1889 received memorials from fifteen presbyteries asking that the Westminster Confession of Faith be revised. But when the Assembly of 1892 submitted proposed revisions to the presbyteries for their approval, not one of the proposed revisions was accepted by the required two thirds of the presbyteries of the church.

The difficult matter of revision was taken up again later with greater success. The General Assembly in 1902 unanimously adopted a "Brief Statement of the Reformed Faith" for a better understanding of our doctrinal beliefs. As this was never submitted to the presbyteries for ratification, it forms no part of the Constitution of the church. In 1903 the church adopted six amendments to the Confession, including new chapters entitled "Of the Holy Spirit" and "Of the Love of God and Missions," as well as a "Declaratory Statement," which asserted God's love for all mankind and also the salvation of all dying in infancy.

Amid extensive changes that were taking place in European and American patterns of thinking, it was becoming increasingly necessary for Christians to state the deepest truths of the gospel in language and in thought forms that would deal creatively with the new ideas, and would at the same time be true to the realities of Christianity. At every new stage of Christian history this restatement of Christian truth has been a necessary though dangerous task. In America there was fear—not entirely unwarranted—that essentials of Christianity were in danger, and in 1909 a series of twelve booklets entitled *The Fundamentals: A Testimony to the Truth* began to be published. The volumes set forth five doctrines as fundamental Christian truths: the virgin birth of Christ, the physical resurrection, the inerrancy of the Scriptures, the substitutionary atonement, and Christ's imminent physical Second Coming. Two wealthy laymen financed the free distribution of 2,500,000 copies.

In the Presbyterian Church there was widespread and often tense discussion of these issues in the church's newspapers and judicatories. The General Assemblies of 1910, 1916, and 1923 set forth five doctrines as "essential doctrines," but the Assembly of 1927, taking a different view of the matter, declared that the Assembly may not, without the joint action of the presbyteries, single out particular doctrines as "essential" and binding on all ministers. Thus the church declined to adopt the platform of so-called "fundamentalism." Though fundamentalism courageously warned the church of dangers involved in theological change, the times called for more sympathetic understanding of contemporary thought and for more profound analysis of the essence of Christianity than was offered by fundamentalism.

The Church's Social Message. During the same decades that the church was struggling with these theological issues, far-reaching social changes were sweeping over the country. The "industrial revolution," substituting machinery for hand labor, had reached the United States about 1830-1840, but it was after the Civil War that its full effects began to be felt. Workingmen, no longer owning their own tools and not yet organized, were economically helpless. Hours were long, wages low, and working conditions often dangerous and unsanitary. Mass movements to the cities created depressing and crime-breeding slums. Unprecedented numbers of immigrants, now mostly of foreign language and non-Protestant, could not be immediately assimilated.

The new conditions caught the churches off balance. American Christians, under the influence of political and economic individualism, and under the influence of the frontier and of revivalism, had come to think that the only responsibility of the Christian church was to save the souls of individuals. But medieval Christians, and the Reformed and Anglican churches, and the early New England Puritans had held the much larger ideal that the Christian church has responsibilities to society as a whole as well as to individuals. The new conditions made it morally necessary for the American churches to reassert their larger responsibilities.

A Presbyterian businessman, Stephen Colwell, had pioneered in 1854 by writing *New Themes for the Protestant Clergy,* in which he criticized the church for its forgetfulness of Christian love and for its failure to denounce contemporary covetousness as sin. But most writers in Presbyterian and other religious periodicals in the 1880's and 1890's were still inclined to the view that a man should be allowed to run his business as he liked, and to look upon those who pressed for larger rights for workingmen as disturbers of the peace. In 1903, however, the Presbyterian Church created a Workingmen's Department, and sponsored the Labor Temple in New York City. The General Assembly in 1910 offered to industry a series of moral goals that it clarified and expanded in succeeding years. The church was recovering its heritage and reasserting that the Christian church has the prophetic task of reminding men that whenever human values are involved, there God's will and God's judgment are to be found.

Meanwhile, before the end of the nineteenth century, Presbyterians were attempting to reach unchurched urban dwellers by evangelism and by institutional churches and neighborhood houses. In Philadelphia, tent evangelistic services regularly drew hundreds of recently arrived Italians. In Chicago and other cities Presbyterian neighborhood houses and settlement houses provided diversified programs of entertainment, instruction, and worship in the spirit of Christian good will. The Board of Home Missions did Christian work in many languages among recent immigrants.

The rush to the cities brought a corresponding depletion of rural areas. As part of his conservation program, President Theodore Roosevelt appointed a Country Life Commission, which reported recommendations in 1908. At about the same time others made sociological studies of the declining rural church, and in 1910 the Presbyterian Board of Home Missions created a Department of the Church and Country Life. Under the able Warren H. Wilson, this Department, by using the best sociological knowledge and techniques, helped many rural churches to greater Christian effectiveness.

Christian Unity. By the late nineteenth century many forces were working to bring the American churches closer together. Some two centuries in the common American environment had developed numerous resemblances and had rubbed off many inherited differences, including many theological differences. The unusually divided state of the American churches in the face of the vast home and foreign missionary task confronting them cried aloud for closer unity, at a time when unity was rapidly increasing in the country's political and economic life. Since early in the nineteenth century, there had been renewed emphasis on the church. This now found increasing expression in co-operation and union among churches as churches, and not merely among Christian individuals as in the earlier days of the "Benevolent Empire" (see Chapter IX).

Presbyterians, in this period between 1869 and the 1930's, were active in all three kinds of Christian unity—nondenominational co-operation of Christian individuals, church federations, and church mergers. The Presbyterian Church acted with Presbyterian and Reformed Churches of many lands to form in 1875 an important federation, the World Presbyterian Alliance. In 1908 the Presbyterian and about thirty other American churches, with some 17,000,000 communicant members, organized the Federal Council of the Churches of Christ in America. Presbyterians were active, too, in working for church mergers. Negotiations were conducted with the Southern Presbyterians, the United Presbyterians, the Episcopalians, and others. In 1918 the General Assembly declared its "profound conviction that the time has come for organic church union of the evangelical churches of America." Eighteen denominations responded, and a Plan of Union creating "The United Churches of Christ in America" was drafted, but failed of adoption.

Presbyterians did enter into two important mergers during this period, however. In 1906 the Cumberland Presbyterian Church, which had separated in 1810 (see Chapter VIII), reunited with the Presbyterian Church U.S.A. though a minority continued its separate existence. The Cumberland Church's chief strength was in the Border States and in the South, and preparatory to the union the Presbyterian Church amended its Constitution to permit organization of separate Negro presbyteries and synods. This was barely forty years after Emancipation, but more advanced ideals of racial integration half a century later made the church eager to restudy this provision. This addition of numerous congregations in the South restored to the Presbyterian Church the national character that it had lost at the time of the Civil War. The Presbyterian Church U.S.A. thus became once again a "national" rather than a merely "Northern" church.

The other organic union was with the Welsh Calvinistic Methodist or Presbyterian Church in the United States. In 1828 the first Welsh Calvinistic Methodist presbytery in the United States was organized. In 1870 this church, which was a true descendant of the church of the same name in Wales, erected a General Assembly and in 1920 merged with the Presbyterian Church in the U.S.A.

Public Worship. Early English Puritanism, in its controversy with Anglicanism, as we have seen, went far beyond the Reformed

Churches of the European continent in its desire for simplicity of worship. For the beautiful medieval cathedrals and churches were substituted bare meetinghouses; embellishments of painting and sculpture and stained glass were cast out in disdain; elaborate and beautiful ritual was scorned as a spiritual distraction and a snare to the soul. In America this Puritan movement toward simplicity in worship was carried even farther under the influence of rude frontier conditions and of emotional revivalism until public worship had become almost slovenly.

Reawakened churchliness in the nineteenth century, however, led some American Presbyterians to new interest in the early Reformed liturgies. A Church Service Society, organized in the home of Dr. Henry van Dyke in 1897, sought to encourage among Presbyterians worthier ideals of public worship. The new interest bore fruit in 1906 in *The Book of Common Worship,* published under the auspices of the General Assembly for voluntary use in the churches. The book was revised in 1932 and 1946 and contains orders of service for public worship, prayers, and forms for many special occasions. It is a definite step in the direction of greater dignity and beauty of worship.

Reorganization of the Boards. In order to promote efficiency and economy of administration, the General Assembly of 1920 appointed a Special Committee on Reorganization and Consolidation of Assembly Agencies. Two years later this committee recommended that the Assembly's sixteen boards and agencies be reorganized into the Office of the General Assembly, the General Council, and four boards, namely, the Board of National Missions, the Board of Foreign Missions, the Board of Christian Education, and the Board of Ministerial Relief and Sustentation. These recommendations were adopted, and became effective in 1923.

The old boards and agencies which were combined to form the new Board of National Missions, with their dates of original establishment, were as follows: the Board of Home Missions (1816), the Woman's Board of Home Missions (1879), the Board of the Church Erection Fund (1844), the Board of Missions for Freedmen (1865), the Permanent Committee on Evangelism (1901), and such work of the Board of Publication and Sabbath School Work as pertained to

its missionary and evangelistic work. This Board today consists of
fifty-four members. There is an executive committee composed of
eighteen members. In addition to these members, whose service is
supervisory and voluntary, there is a salaried staff, headed by a general secretary. The other three Boards are organized on somewhat
similar lines, but differ in size of membership.

The Board of National Missions today does Christian work among
mountaineers, Indians, Negroes, Orientals, Jews, and many foreign
language groups, by maintaining Christian workers, churches, Sunday
church schools, schools, and hospitals. It aids needy churches in both
urban and rural fields, supplementing both salaries and building
funds. Through the church judicatories, through special conferences,
and by direct correspondence with pastors, its Division of Evangelism, under the guidance of the Church's National Commission on
Evangelism, seeks to promote Christian commitment and life
throughout the church.

The present Board of Foreign Missions was formed by the com-
bination of the Board of Foreign Missions (established 1837) and
the Woman's Board of Foreign Missions (established 1870). This
Board is today operating in twenty-one nations or areas of the world:
Africa (the Cameroun), Brazil, Chile, China (Taiwan and Hong
Kong), Colombia, Europe, Guatemala, India, Indonesia, Iran, Iraq,
Japan, Korea, Lebanon, Mexico, Pakistan, the Philippines, Syria,
Thailand, United Andean Indian Mission, and Venezuela. The amazing expansion of foreign missionary activity has perhaps been the
most significant event in Protestant Christianity since the beginning
of the nineteenth century. The Presbyterian Church in the United
States of America, through its Board of Foreign Missions, has been
an outstanding leader of this movement.

The following were the boards and agencies, with their dates of
original establishment, which merged in 1923 to form the Board
of Christian Education: the General Board of Education (1819), the
Board of Publication and Sabbath School Work (1838), the Board of
Temperance and Moral Welfare (1881), the Permanent Committee
on Men's Work (1913), and the Permanent Committee on Sabbath
Observance (1919).

The Board of Christian Education publishes an extensive religious literature, a large part of which is in the form of church school lesson materials. This Board seeks to aid the church in the training of consecrated volunteer leaders. It helps in the maintenance of Christian colleges and co-operates with Christian forces in "secular" colleges and universities. It offers needed financial assistance for students preparing for the ministry and other forms of full-time Christian service. To this Board is also entrusted the task of fostering in the church, by promotional and educational acitivity: Christian ideals of the home; true principles of Christian stewardship; a quickened social conscience; a growing zeal for missions; and a deepening of the spiritual life of pastors and parishioners alike. The task of this Board, it will be seen, is very closely related to that of the Board of National Missions at many points, and an Interboard Commission on National Missions and Christian Education has been erected to aid in coordinating their work. These two Boards, under the supervision of the General Assembly, are laboring earnestly together to make the church more truly spiritual and to make America more truly Christian.

The Board of Ministerial Relief had been formally established in 1855. In 1912 it combined with the Ministerial Sustentation Fund to form the Board of Ministerial Relief and Sustentation. The consolidation of 1923 erected this into one of the four separate church Boards, the name of which, in 1928, was changed to the Board of Pensions. In 1927 a Pension Plan for ministers and nonministerial salaried church workers was set up under this Board.

The creation of the General Council was part of the plan of reorganization. This came into existence in 1923, and superseded the New Era and Every Member Plan Committees and the Executive Commission. Its chief task is to co-ordinate and expedite the work of the four Boards.

The Office of the General Assembly, of which the Stated Clerk of the General Assembly is the executive head, today contains three departments: Administration, Publicity, and History.

CHAPTER XII

Recent Trends

The New Orthodoxy. Starting in the mid-1930's, "neo-orthodoxy" began to influence Christian thinking in America. Men had been so busy analyzing the physical universe and building machines that some thought that the only kind of reality must be a rational system—like the physical universe, for example, which man's reason had analyzed, or like a machine developed by man's reason. Some, especially in Europe, were speaking of modern times as "de-Christianized" or as "the post-Christian era." Meanwhile some philosophers in the nineteenth century had been saying that man's existence is more than his reasoning power, and that in order to maintain his existence man must continually make decisions and assert his will.

In 1919, amid the despair and agony that followed World War I in Europe, Karl Barth declared that the important thing for man is to face the basal fact of his existence—that he is a guilty sinner and must make a right decision about God. In the spirit of the Protestant Reformation this "neo-orthodoxy" insisted that Christian life is personal encounter with God and trust in him as revealed in Jesus Christ. It taught that the Bible is the record of God's revelation of himself, which the Holy Spirit causes to become the Word of God to the individual believer.

It was in the 1930's, when American self-confidence was prostrated by the great depression, that neo-orthodoxy entered the Presbyterian and other American churches. It came just as the rather futile "fundamentalist-modernist" controversy was waning, and offered a kind of "middle ground" on which extremists might unite. It accepted without fear the conclusions of modern critical scholarship in Biblical and other fields but insisted on the reality of man's sin, God's revelation, the incarnation in Christ, and redemption through him. Neo-orthodoxy has been much criticized, often deservedly so, but it has been a breath of new life to Christian thinking in Europe and America. In Presbyterian classrooms, pulpits, and pews it has contributed to renewed interest in Christian truth.

The Ecumenical Movement. The word "ecumenical" is from a Greek word meaning "the whole inhabited world," or "world-wide." The ecumenical movement is not trying to organize a superchurch, but to realize spiritual oneness among Christians throughout the world in fulfillment of Christ's prayer in John 17: 21: "That they may all be one."

The modern ecumenical movement has three principal roots: foreign missions, the application of Christian principles to social problems (called the "Life and Work" movement), and the search for theological agreement (called the "Faith and Order" movement).

Foreign missions, before the opening of the twentieth century, had planted the Christian church in every major area of the world. Co-operation among missionary boards and mergers among the younger churches on the field were pointing the way toward Christian unity on a world-wide basis. The World Missionary Conference at Edinburgh in 1910 was a milestone. Hundreds of scholars from many lands prepared studies for it, and its Continuation Committee paved the way for organizing the International Missionary Council in 1921, which continuously views the missionary enterprise in terms of a single global Christian strategy.

Missionary [margin annotation]

The Life and Work movement tried to enlist the wisdom and resources of the churches of the world in order that they might unitedly give Christian guidance to the great social forces, international and domestic, that are remaking modern life. Life and Work took form at a conference in Stockholm, Sweden, in 1925, and was further developed in a conference at Oxford, England, in 1937.

Social [margin annotation]

The third root of the ecumenical movement, the Faith and Order movement, heroically addressed itself to a full and frank discussion of the theological issues that keep the churches divided, as well as of the truths that Christians hold in common. Faith and Order held

Theological [margin annotation]

its first conference at Lausanne, Switzerland, in 1927, with a later conference at Edinburgh, Scotland, in 1937. The two movements— Life and Work and Faith and Order—combined to form, at Amsterdam, Holland, in 1948, the World Council of Churches, with more than 150 member churches. The World Council held its second assembly at Evanston, Illinois, in 1954.

The Presbyterian Church has contributed important leadership and support to all three branches of the ecumenical movement from their beginning. Today one cannot be a good Presbyterian without being an earnest world Christian. On national and local levels, Presbyterians have shown their ecumenical spirit, among other ways, by helping, in 1950, to combine eight federations to form the National Council of the Churches of Christ in the U.S.A.; by participating actively in numerous state and local federations and co-operative undertakings; and by amending their Constitution frequently to endorse and facilitate Christian unity. As the world is torn by change and animosities, the Christian churches are increasingly trying to provide spiritual healing and unity.

The Church's World Mission. World War II fanned into a flame the revolt of peoples in Asia and Africa against colonialism. Nations just born struggled heroically against imperialism, poverty, and illiteracy. To anxious millions the siren voice of Russian communism promised emancipation and power. In some areas, Roman Catholic intolerance and in others the reinvigoration of non-Christian religions posed further problems for Protestant missions. Meanwhile, as a vigorous new Christianity was arising among "non-Christian" nations, a deadly paganism from within was threatening the so-called "Christian" nations. Thus by mid-twentieth century the whole idea of missions had changed. It was now realized that older and younger churches were partners in a single task—that of bearing witness to the saving power of Jesus Christ against unbelief and paganism in every nation of the world.

The Presbyterian Church streamlined its missionary strategy to meet the new situation, especially the rising nationalism. Earlier tendencies to encourage the younger churches to become "self-governing, self-supporting, and self-propagating" were speeded up.

"Missions" were transformed into national churches, with "missionaries" in such churches taking the new name "fraternal workers," who acted in an advisory capacity while the nationals took over direct leadership. These changes were strikingly reflected in the *Presbyterian Year Book of Prayer for Missions 1957*, where the names of 250 nationals were listed. Leaders of churches overseas were secured, too, for service on the executive staff of the Presbyterian Board of Foreign Missions.

The new needs and methods were conspicuous in the World Consultation conducted by the Presbyterian Board of Foreign Missions at Lake Mohonk, New York, in the spring of 1956. Of the 129 delegates, 25 were nationals from Asia, Africa, and Latin America, and 24 were missionaries and field representatives of the Board. The Consultation urged the rapid transformation of missions into national churches and proposed as the two top priorities evangelism and the raising up of Christian leaders. At the same time an increased number of American missionaries was urgently desired.

Missionary education and promotion at home was carefully planned. By 1957 about a quarter of American Presbyterian churches directed their foreign missionary support to specific projects abroad, thus giving church members increased knowledge of and interest in the work. Many were in the "Parish to Parish Plan" whereby American congregations were directly related to congregations overseas. Filmstrips, the Board's lending library, periodical and other literature, speakers in churches, and more than a hundred radio and television programs annually helped to keep the church informed.

Even amid world upheaval, the 1,004 Presbyterian missionary and fraternal workers in 1955 could see many signs of promise. In spite of terrible war losses, the Korean Church had doubled in size within a decade. Brazil had the largest Latin Protestant community in the world. In Mexico 8 per cent of the population had become Protestant. In some Moslem lands the church was making a renewed thrust. Christian work was advancing encouragingly in the Philippines, Thailand, Africa, and in many other fields.

Social Concern. The economic depression of the 1930's, which brought widespread unemployment and suffering, focused attention on serious defects in the American economic system, and caused the General Assembly to take more advanced ground in its economic pronouncements. The Department of Social Education and Action, created by the Board of Christian Education in 1936, gave to the church important leadership in this and other social fields. In 1944, during the economic pressures of World War II, the Assembly voiced large Christian views on industrial relations, confessing the church's economic and social sins, and asserting the obligation of Christians to foster in economic pressure groups—such as industry, labor, agriculture, consumers—a desire to serve the welfare of all.

Vast population movements within the country, increased by migration of workers to defense plants during World War II but continuing after the war, created problems for the church. Cities continued to expand, not only in the Northeastern and North Central States but on the Pacific Coast and in the South. Large housing projects became a new mission field. The problem of the decay and renewal of downtown areas, the "inner city," was particularly acute, and in 1954 the Board of National Missions appointed a Special Committee on the Inner City. As the movement away from farms continued, Presbyterians made increasing use of the "Larger Parish Plan," in which nearby rural congregations combined forces to secure a staff of ministers performing specialized functions. Among the promising areas of America to enjoy development in this era was Alaska, where the Board of National Missions was aiding some thirty churches.

On the issue of peace and war, Presbyterians shared the fluctuations and spiritual growing pains of the country as a whole. Presbyterians had endorsed World War I, in the language of the Confession of Faith, as "just and necessary," while many prominent Presbyterians became enthusiastic for the fray as a great moral crusade. But for Presbyterians as for others disillusionment followed. Having heartily and unsuccessfully supported the League of Nations previously, the Assembly in 1934 announced "its break with the entire war system" and declared that "Christians cannot give their support to war as a method of carrying on international conflict." Much in this spirit, an amendment was proposed to the church's Constitution emphasizing the individual's conscience and removing the statement that the civil government has the right to wage war. The amendment failed of adoption in 1939.

In World War II the church endorsed the war as necessary, but tried at the same time to keep in mind the obligations of Christian humility and charity. Toward the close of the war the church was active in a World Order Movement, which helped to create in the United States a climate congenial to the formation of the United Nations. Amid the birth pangs of a new era, Presbyterians tried increasingly, though imperfectly, to be guided by the standards of revealed truth, rather than by the mob passions of the moment. The war was the occasion of important chaplain and relief services, and following the war, a Restoration Fund of more than $23,000,000 was raised for reconstruction and new Christian work. In the "cold war" against communistic Russia which followed, the General Council by "A Letter to Presbyterians," in 1953, spoke vigorously and courageously for freedom and justice against an enslaving fear of communism that was sweeping the country.

The churches, like American secular institutions, have been deeply involved in racial segregation. But by the 1950's the situation was giving them acute pangs of conscience and there were signs of promise. In 1954 the General Assembly appointed a Special Committee to confer with the synods and presbyteries of the church that were organized on the basis of race or language, and two years later the Assembly approved the merger of the Synod of Oklahoma and the former Negro Synod of Canadian. A few congregations were becoming integrated and a very few were being served by an interracial ministry. At least a beginning was being made in "operation desegregation."

Women's Work. One of the interesting developments since the Presbyterian reunion of 1869, and particularly in most recent years, has been the increasingly prominent position officially accorded to women in the work of the Presbyterian Church. In 1870 the Woman's Foreign Missionary Society was organized in the church, followed, in 1879, by the organization of the Woman's Board of Home Missions. In 1915 an amendment to the Constitution authorized the election of deaconesses. In 1923 women were made eligible to membership on all the denominational Boards and to membership on the General Council, while a Constitutional amendment in 1930 opened to them the office of ruling elder. The office of commissioned church worker, recognized by the church's Constitution in 1948, was from the beginning open to women, and finally in 1956 women were made eligible to the highest office of the church, the ministry.

The Church and Education. A notable achievement of the Presbyterian Church was the launching of its new *Christian Faith and Life* curriculum for church schools in October, 1948. Utilizing the co-operation of parents for homework, it issued attractively illustrated and designed materials, many of them as bound books. In recurring three-year cycles it dealt with the themes Christ, the Bible, the Christian church. Possessing ecumenical outlook and strong missionary interest, the curriculum had the evangelical emphasis of personal commitment to Christ. By 1956 the materials were being used in three quarters of the church's schools and portions had been translated into nine languages and dialects.

A notable addition to religious journalism in America was *Presbyterian Life*. Starting in 1949 with a circulation of 80,982, by the summer of 1957 it had a list of regular subscribers that passed the million mark. Written in an ecumenical spirit, avoiding a too narrow denominationalism, and with its interesting pictures, attractive format, and popularly written articles, it has helped to keep Presbyterians everywhere informed on the work of the Kingdom.

Presbyterian church school enrollment reflected the often-mentioned religious awakening of these years, increasing by more than one third in the decade following World War II—nearly three times as much as the rate of population increase. The church expanded its lay leadership-training programs and increased the number of directors of Christian education in the local churches to nearly 800. In 1945 the General Assembly approved Westminster Fellowship as the official denominational program for young people from twelve to twenty-three years of age. Summer conferences and camps expanded to reach more than 45,000 young people in 1956, giving instruction and recreation, and inspiring many to choose Christian service vocations.

The characteristic interest of Presbyterians in education has increased rather than diminished with the years. In 1956 forty-one colleges were affiliated with the Presbyterian Church, with an enrollment of nearly 30,000 students and an investment of more than $143,000,000. The Board of Christian Education represents the church in relations with the colleges, and a Presbyterian College Union also fosters their common interests. In addition, Presbyterian Westminster Foundations were conducting Christian work on 144 non-Presbyterian campuses, ministering to as many as possible of the estimated quarter million Presbyterian youth in the secular colleges and universities of the land.

The church's program of adult work—much of it administrative and functional rather than educational in character—has developed greatly. A National Council of Women's Organizations meets every four years to give leadership and guidance to the women's work in the local churches, presbyteries, and synods. Men of the church organized a National Council of Presbyterian Men in 1948 which grew from 177 chapters at the end of the first year to 2,516 chapters seven years later. The Council, which is composed of lay representatives from the church's presbyteries, boards, and agencies, and of ministerial representatives from the synods, seeks to encourage Presbyterian men to organize for the work of the church on the local, presbyterial, and national levels.

The church showed increasing interest in educating its candidates for the ministry. Starting in 1941, the theological seminaries received a percentage of the church's total benevolence giving. A Council of Theological Education was organized in 1943 under the authority of the General Assembly, with representatives from all of the seminaries and Boards, and also representatives from the church at large. Its purpose was to call the attention of the church to the needs of the seminaries, to help the seminaries to co-operate with one another, and to relate their work as closely as possible to the church. This tightening of relations between church and seminaries has proved mutually valuable. Reflecting perhaps a general quickening of religious interest in the church and nation, the seminaries as a whole experienced a substantial increase in enrollment. Changing times brought changes in curriculum with further changes in prospect, such as supervision and expansion of field work and new interest in pastoral counseling.

The Church Today. This brings to a close the story of the Presbyterian Church in the United States of America, briefly sketched in Chapters VI-XII.

The most apparent change since the early days of Francis Makemie was of course that of physical growth. The church as first organized had one presbytery with seven ministers, and scattered churches in Maryland, Delaware, and Philadelphia. The church in 1956 had 10,323 ministers, 8,658 churches, and 2,809,603 communicant members, organized in 250 presbyteries and 39 synods, under one General Assembly. Instead of being confined to a part of three colonies, it was spread across a continent having churches in every state of the union, with mission stations throughout the world.

In its physical equipment, the church progressed almost beyond recognition. Its worship tended away from Puritan rigor toward the greater employment of the beautiful. Minor amendments of its standards of doctrine and polity had been made. Great indeed were the changes in the atmosphere of its thinking. It shared the newer emphasis on God's love, and a resulting quickened missionary zeal. As the church in 1957 entered a new church union and took a new name, the divine pillar of fire and cloud was still going on before, pointing the church forward and onward to greater achievements for Christ.

CHAPTER XIII

The United Presbyterian Church of North America

Ancestors of the United Presbyterian Church of North America. In 1957 the Presbyterian Church in the United States of America and the United Presbyterian Church of North America merged to form the United Presbyterian Church in the United States of America. Chapters VI-XII have dealt with the history of the Presbyterian Church in the U.S.A. The present chapter will sketch the history of the United Presbyterian Church of North America.

The United Presbyterian Church of North America has been the principal representative in our country of the Scottish "dissenting" churches, that is, the "Covenanters" and the "Seceders" (see Chapter IV). This has been a difficult as well as an important role. The Scottish Covenants and other special issues that gave birth to these churches were rooted in Scottish life and could not easily be transplanted to America. The struggles in Scotland had stimulated strong convictions and independence of spirit. These qualities, in spite of the fact that the groups in America were unusually homogeneous in nationality and beliefs, for a long time made unity among them very difficult. The story of the United Presbyterian Church of North America is in brief the story of successfully uniting and preserving this heroic heritage and of relating it to contemporary American life.

Scattered Covenanters and Seceders from both Scotland and northern Ireland settled in New York, southeastern Pennsylvania, and South Carolina, and later moved west, western Pennsylvania eventually becoming their chief stronghold. In a colorful ceremony at

Middle Octorara, Pennsylvania, in 1743, Covenanters "renewed the Covenants" with drawn swords, reminding them of the perils faced by their ancestors in the days of Charles II and James II. John Cuthbertson, first Covenanter minister to settle in the colonies, came in 1751. He traveled on horseback some 70,000 miles through forests and across rivers, in danger of Indians and wild animals, sometimes sleeping outdoors in rain or snow, preaching, counseling, administering the sacraments, exercising church discipline. "Tired but safe," he wrote in his diary at the end of a busy day. In 1774, with two other Covenanter ministers, Cuthbertson organized the Reformed Presbytery of America. In 1753, the Seceders, the other principal root of the United Presbyterian Church of North America, organized under the name Associate Presbytery of Pennsylvania.

In the Revolutionary War, Covenanters and Seceders ardently supported the patriot side. If they could unite in supporting American independence, why not unite in one church, which would be independent of the church bodies and historic controversies of the mother country? This was done, and in 1782 Covenanters and Seceders united to form the Associate Reformed Church.

The union was a statesmanlike one, but it faced many difficulties. Some Covenanters and some Seceders declined to enter the union and continued their independent bodies. In the 1820's, for geographical as well as ecclesiastical reasons, the Associate Reformed Church itself divided into a number of independent bodies. Its Synod of Carolina organized what has since become the General Synod of the Associate Reformed Presbyterian Church, located in the South. Another portion united with the Presbyterian Church in the U.S.A. But the larger part of the church reunited in 1856 to constitute the General Synod of the Associate Reformed Church.

The Formation of the United Presbyterian Church of North America. A new day dawned for the family of Scottish dissenting churches with the formation of the United Presbyterian Church of North America in 1858. Differences over methods of defining the distinctive beliefs that these churches held in common almost wrecked union hopes. But laymen were eager for closer co-operation, and union triumphed. On May 26, 1858, delegates of the General

Synod of the Associate Reformed Church met delegates from the Synod of the Associate Presbyterian Church (Seceders) at Seventh and Smithfield Streets in what is now Pittsburgh's "golden triangle" and marched together to the old City Hall to celebrate the union of these two churches to form the United Presbyterian Church of North America. Reformed Presbyterians (Covenanters) who had declined to accompany other Covenanters into the earlier union of 1782 had negotiated for a time, but once again remained separate. Thus, by mid-twentieth century, except for the Associate Reformed Presbyterian Church, with a membership of 27,467 located in the South and the Reformed Presbyterian Church in North America (General Synod), with 1,279 members, and the Reformed Presbyterian Church of North America (Old School), with 6,382 members, and the Associate Presbyterian Church of North America, with 470, the United Presbyterian Church of North America, with its membership of 251,344, included all the direct ecclesiastical heirs in America of Covenanters and Seceders.

Those who were about to unite in 1858 held two conventions in the months before the union. Covenanters and Seceders were strict in their orthodoxy and had a deep devotional quality in their personal faith, but had never been identified with American revivalism. The religious revival of 1857-1858 (see Chapter X), however, was at the moment filling many of their congregations, and was conspicuous in these conventions. Many in convention confessed the churches' sins, including the sin of disunity, and in prolonged discussions inquired how the churches, by Biblical rather than by sensational methods, might receive God's fullest blessing. These earnest meetings did much to set the tone of the union of 1858 and of the United Presbyterian Church of North America, which was there formed.

The basis for the union of 1858 was the Westminster Confession of Faith, the Larger and Shorter Catechisms, and a "Judicial Testimony" consisting of eighteen declarations, the last five of which set forth the new church's "distinctives," that is, the particular views that distinguished it (and its predecessors) from other churches. The five "distinctives" were: (1) opposition to slavery; (2) refusal to admit to communicant membership members of oathbound secret societies; (3) invitation to the Lord's Supper restricted to those who adhere to the church's distinctive tenets; (4) endorsement of the principle of covenanting; and (5) the exclusive use of the psalms for singing in worship. The slavery issue ended with the Civil War, and the other four "distinctives" were officially abandoned in 1925.

Developments Since 1858. Hardly was the United Presbyterian Church of North America created in 1858 before the Civil War was upon the country. With the distinguished antislavery record of its parent churches, the new church in 1863 undertook work among some 10,000 Negro refugees who had sought freedom behind Federal army lines in Nashville, Tennessee. Like all refugees, they lacked homes, clothing, food. Within a month, the United Presbyterian missionary, Rev. Joseph G. McKee, was ministering to the sick, supplying the necessities of life, and had opened a school to which old and young flocked. In 1875 Knoxville College was founded for "Freedmen" in Knoxville, Tennessee. The church's work for Negroes has since expanded to include churches and schools in Kentucky, Tennessee, Virginia, North Carolina, and Alabama.

The women of the church have done notable work, starting a Women's General Missionary Society in 1883 which was active in nearly every area of the church's home and foreign missions. In 1888 this Society created an Annual Thank-offering, which over the years raised hundreds of thousands of dollars. After the rise of Christian Endeavor and of local young people's societies, the church in 1889 held the first national convention of its Young People's Christian Union. In more recent years the program was reconstructed along age group lines. The church has two colleges in Egypt and one in Pakistan, in addition to six in the United States: Muskingum in Ohio (founded in 1837), Westminster in Pennsylvania (1852), Monmouth in Illinois (1853), Knoxville in Tennessee (1875), Tarkio in Missouri (1883), and Sterling in Kansas (1887). The church also has three theological seminaries: Pittsburgh-Xenia in Pittsburgh, which has early roots in both of the parent churches, and seminaries in Cairo, Egypt, and Gujranwala, Pakistan.

By a series of Board consolidations starting in 1923, the church reduced its Boards to five: Administration (for co-ordinating and promoting the general work of the church), American Missions (formerly Home Missions), Foreign Missions, Christian Education, and Ministerial Pensions and Relief. The Board of American Missions and its predecessors, in addition to aiding young and needy churches, through the years developed such diversified service as work among Mormons (started in 1904), Sunday School missions (1908), work among mountaineers (1908) and among immigrants (1909), evangelism (1909), social service (1911), church erection (1923).

In 1854 the Associate Presbyterian Synod had elected Andrew Gordon to be its pioneer missionary to India. Others had declined appointment, but Gordon and his young wife accepted heartily as a call from God. Sailing on a freighter on which they had to build their own bunks, they reached India early in 1855. It took two years to win three converts. But the work grew and prospered. In 1854 the Associate Reformed Church had started missionary work in Egypt. The United Presbyterian Church inherited and enlarged these beginnings until work was carried on in five lands abroad: India, Pakistan, Egypt, The Sudan (begun in 1900), and Abyssinia (1919). The home church has maintained unusually close relations with the foreign field and has consistently been among the highest of American churches in per capita gifts to missions. Nearly a quarter of the church's membership is in Asia and Africa, and its second largest synod is in Pakistan.

The first General Assembly after World War I, in 1919, voted unanimously to prepare a revised Statement of Faith as a part of the "reconstruction duty" of "the new era." It was felt that the Westminster Confession was "falling into disuse" and did not in every detail represent the church's contemporary beliefs, so that subscription to it was "commonly accompanied with reservations." A Confessional Statement, which summarized in clear modern language and which slightly modified the teaching of the Westminster Confession, was adopted in 1924 and 1925. The Preamble to it says, "This Statement . . . takes the place of the Testimony of 1858, and wherever it deviates from the Westminster Standards its declarations are to prevail."

The Statement was an important milestone in the church's history. By replacing the Judicial Testimony of 1858 it officially discarded

the church's "distinctives," and opened the way for closer fellowship
and unity with other Christian churches. This Statement showed,
too, that the church's venerable heritage of "Covenants" and later
of written "Testimonies," while originally having the effect of making
the Confession tighter and stricter, could be used in the opposite direction of a vigorous progressivism. The inherited ideal of the church's
living voice was finding new expression.

The ideal of Christian unity played a conspicuous and growing
role in the history of the United Presbyterians. In the century before
1858, their parent churches struggled unsuccessfully for durable
unity among themselves in the face of detailed, conscientious differences. The union of 1858, which created the United Presbyterian
Church of North America, was a major turning point. During three
quarters of the years from 1858 until 1957 this church was actively
negotiating some church union. In the nineteenth century, conversa-
tions were usually with smaller Presbyterian and Reformed bodies,
whereas in the twentieth century extended negotiations were conducted with larger bodies also, some of the proposals being to unite
simultaneously with more than one church.

In 1910, as one of the earlier church bodies to take such action,
the General Assembly set up a Permanent Committee on Church Relations to guide the church in co-operation and union. The United
Presbyterians were members of the World Presbyterian Alliance, the
National Council of Churches, and the World Council of Churches.
The church's history is a dynamic one. It is the story of a body of
Christians with strong and precisely defined convictions who peri-
odically, after searching discussion, related anew their heritage to
changing American conditions.

The United Presbyterian Church in the U.S.A. An important union
of American Presbyterian bodies occurred in 1957 when the Presbyterian Church in the U.S.A. and the United Presbyterian Church of
North America voted to merge under the name of the United Presbyterian Church in the U.S.A., this merger to be consummated in
Pittsburgh on May 28, 1958. There had been intermittent talk of
such a union since soon after the Civil War, a concerted mutual
effort toward it in 1934, and continuous official negotiations since

1951, when a three-way union including also the Southern Presbyterians was being considered. When this three-way union did not materialize, the two General Assemblies in 1955 authorized the drafting of a Plan of Union to unite the two churches, and the next year submitted the finished Plan to their respective presbyteries. The presbyteries approved, and the two Assemblies gave final confirmation in 1957. As in Scotland in 1929, heirs of Scottish establishment and dissent were at last reunited.

The new church's Constitution consists of three doctrinal standards: The Westminster Confession of Faith and the Larger and Shorter Catechisms; and of three governmental standards: the Directory for the Worship of God, the Form of Government, and the Book of Discipline—all six embodying the historic faith and practice of the two churches. A Special Committee on Consolidations was set up to recommend in due time appropriate consolidation of synods and presbyteries and of boards, agencies, and other institutions of the two churches.

The presbyteries and General Assembly of the Presbyterian Church in the U.S.A. favored union almost unanimously. The General Assembly of the United Presbyterian Church, after a divided vote on union, unanimously adopted the following resolution: "It is resolved by the Ninety-ninth General Assembly that we enter into the union of our church and the Presbyterian Church U.S.A. with faith, hope, and love and the prayerful purpose of making the union a happy and effective means of advancing the Kingdom of Jesus Christ, our Savior and Lord." In this spirit the united church looks forward to a larger and greater future under the guidance of God.

CHAPTER XIV

Conclusion

Plan of Conclusion. The interest of the present studies has centered around the Presbyterian Church in the United States of America and the United Presbyterian Church of North America. The first five chapters showed their medieval and modern background in Europe; Chapters VI-XII sketched the history of the Presbyterian Church in the U.S.A.; and Chapter XIII told the history of the United Presbyterian Church of North America. In order that our view may not be too narrowly restricted to these two churches, let us, in this closing chapter, fill out somewhat the picture of the Presbyterian family of churches by referring briefly to the various Presbyterian denominations in the United States; to Presbyterians in other parts of the world; and to underlying principles of Presbyterian polity, doctrine, and worship.

Presbyterian Denominations in the United States. The various Presbyterian denominations in the United States fall naturally into three groups: the Presbyterian Church in the United States of America and those originating from it; those having their origin in the "Covenanter" and "Secession" movements of Scotland; those of Continental origin (Dutch and German).

In the first group of American Presbyterian Churches—the Presbyterian Church in the United States of America and those originating from it—we mention six. By far the largest and the most truly national of all was the *Presbyterian Church in the United States of America* itself, with 2,809,603 communicant members in 1956. Next in size comes the *Presbyterian Church in the United States* (the

"Southern Church"), mentioned in Chapter X, with a membership of 829,570. The *Cumberland Presbyterian Church* separated from the Presbyterian Church in the United States of America in 1810 and reunited with it in 1906, as related in Chapter VIII. But a minority of the Cumberland Church continued a separate existence, and has 85,651 members. The *Cumberland Presbyterian Church (Colored)* has some 30,000 members. The *Orthodox Presbyterian Church* separated from the Presbyterian Church in the U.S.A. in 1936. It originally bore the name "Presbyterian Church of America," but changed this name in 1939. It has 9,200 members. The *Bible Presbyterian Church* separated from the Presbyterian Church of America in 1937.

The American Presbyterian Churches of the second group—those originating in the "Covenanter" and "Secession" movements of Scotland—have been mentioned with statistics in Chapter XIII. The United Presbyterian Church of North America was the largest church in this group.

In the third group of American Presbyterian Churches—those of Continental origin—we mention three. These are the (Dutch) Reformed Church in America, the Christian Reformed Church in North America (also from Holland), and the United Church of Christ.

The Dutch Reformed Church is the oldest Presbyterian organization in America. In 1628, Rev. John Michaelius organized in New Amsterdam its first congregation, which is now the strong Collegiate Church of New York City. The English captured New Amsterdam in 1664, but the use of the Dutch language in many congregations was continued for a long time. In 1785 the church declared its independence of the classis in Holland, and seven years later drew up its constitution. This denomination claims the oldest theological seminary in the United States, as John H. Livingston became a professor of theology in 1784, and in 1810 opened a theological seminary in New Brunswick, New Jersey. In 1867 the church changed its name to the *Reformed Church in America,* omitting the term "Dutch" from the official title. This body has a membership of 208,999. It maintains theological seminaries at New Brunswick, New Jersey, and Holland, Michigan. The church possesses three doctrinal standards: the Belgic Confession, the Canons of the Synod of Dort, and the Heidelberg Catechism.

The *Christian Reformed Church in North America*—the other Presbyterian Church of Dutch origin—is an extremely conservative body that assumed its present form in 1889 by a combination of three groups that had seceded from the Dutch Reformed Church in Holland and America. This church condemns Freemasonry and all oathbound secret societies.

The German Reformed Church was organized in America early in the eighteenth century among German immigrants, most of whom hailed from the Palatinate. In 1747 an American "coetus" was organized, subordinate to the Classis of Amsterdam, in Holland, which was giving generous financial aid. In 1791 the church caught the prevailing spirit of nationalism and declared its ecclesiastical independence. The great tide of German immigration in the nineteenth century brought steady growth. By 1869 the church had become so much Americanized that it dropped the word "German" from its title, and took the name Reformed Church in the United States. In 1934 it formed the Evangelical and Reformed Church by a merger with the Evangelical Synod of North America, a body that was composed of both Lutheran and Reformed elements. In 1957 this Evangelical and Reformed Church, which had 784,270 members, united with the Congregational Christian Churches, which had 1,379,394 members, to form the *United Church of Christ*. This was one of the most important unions in twentieth-century America because it brought together churches of Presbyterian and Congregational church government, and of Continental European (Evangelical and Reformed) and English Puritan (Congregational Christian) heritage.

World-wide Presbyterianism. Let us now take a fleeting glimpse at the Presbyterian churches of the world, most of which, outside of America and Europe, are, or until recently have been, mission churches. Their very existence bears eloquent testimony to Presbyterian missionary zeal.

The Presbyterians of North America—including the churches of Canada and the United States, as well as the *Presbyterian Church in Mexico*—number more than 5,584,000. The Presbyterians of Europe (including both the Continent and the British Isles) number over 5,478,000.

The Presbyterian churches of Africa, which include those of the Union of South Africa, a British dominion, report 1,298,000 members.

Asia, which has been almost exclusively a mission field, now has nearly 900,000 Presbyterians in such vigorous denominations as—to mention only a few—the *Church of Christ* in Japan, the *Presbyterian Church* of Korea, and the *United Church of Christ* in the Philippines.

Some 171,000 Presbyterians are found in Australasia—in the churches of the British dominions, Australia, and New Zealand, as well as in the mission churches of the islands.

In South America, which is nominally Roman Catholic, Presbyterians are doing splendid work, reporting 100,000 communicant members.

The communicant membership of the Presbyterian churches of the world totals over 10,000,000. This means that Presbyterian adherents —in the broader sense—number approximately 40,000,000, constituting one of the largest and most influential Protestant groups of churches in the world.

Presbyterian Principles of Polity, Doctrine, and Worship Summarized. The term "Presbyterian," it should be emphasized, refers not to a particular type of doctrine or worship, but to a particular form of church government—government by presbyters, or elders. There are four types of church government: Papal, corresponding to political absolute monarchy; Episcopal, corresponding to political aristocracy; Presbyterian, or government by elected representatives, corresponding to political republicanism; Congregational, or direct control of church affairs by the members of the congregation, corresponding to political democracy. Presbyterian polity, in its most fully developed form, operates through four graded church "courts," or judicatories: the lowest, a session or consistory; above this, a presbytery or classis; above this, a synod or a particular synod; above this the one General Assembly or General Synod. The Presbyterian judicatories are all composed of both ministers and ruling elders, and exercise legislative and executive and judicial functions.

Correctly speaking, there is no such thing as "Presbyterian" doctrine (or worship either), since the term "Presbyterian" refers to a form of government. But most of the Presbyterian churches adhere, with greater or less strictness, to the system of doctrine associated with the name of John Calvin, in which the sovereignty and supreme will of God receive emphasis. Recent generations of Presbyterians have been interpreting this truth in terms of God's loving will.

As to worship, individual church sessions have large freedom. As a result, little can be said concerning Presbyterian worship that is universally valid. The Presbyterians of the European continent have tended toward a somewhat more formal ritual, the British and American Presbyterians, influenced by Puritanism, toward a less formal. Today, however, many Presbyterian congregations of America are leaning toward greater elaboration and "enrichment" of ritual. This remains a matter within the discretion of each local session subject to the requirements of the Directory for Worship. It is, however, being increasingly recognized that, amid change and variety, Presbyterian worship must maintain what was central for the fathers of the Reformed faith, namely, theological integrity. That is, it must be consistent with God's revealed truth.

Finis. In these brief studies we have seen the little church planted by Jesus Christ become a world force. We have seen it broken into countless separate "churches," and have traced briefly the outline of one of the most important groups of churches, the Presbyterian. Presbyterians are only a part of the Kingdom, but they have their valuable contribution to make to the common work for the Master. Pending the day of closer co-operation, let each group serve the Christ faithfully with the special talents and heritage it has received. So will the common task of all prosper most, and the Kingdom be most surely advanced.

QUESTIONS AND BIBLIOGRAPHY

Questions for Thought and Discussion

CHAPTER I

In what sense might Presbyterianism be said to be as old as the apostles?

Could the early Christian martyrs have escaped death? How?

Were the conversion of the emperor and the official recognition of Christianity a gain or a loss for the Christian church? Give reasons.

What great military movement marks the beginning of the Middle Ages? What service did the Christian church perform amidst the confusion of those invasions?

Name some of the good effects of the papacy in its early days; some of its bad effects later.

What were the motives that caused people to go into monasteries?

Does the fact that Christ founded the church keep it free from error? Does the Christian church today need reform? Does it need revival?

CHAPTER II

Was Martin Luther right or wrong when he taught that a person's soul is saved by faith alone?

Does God today expect us to follow our individual consciences in preference to the commands of church and governmental authorities as Martin Luther did at the Diet of Worms? On the other hand, should we be willing to sacrifice for social convenience whims not based on intelligent conscience? What place does the Bible have in helping us to distinguish between true "conscience" and mere whim?

Was Calvin correct in thinking of Christianity as a direct relationship to Christ as a living Person?

What do you think of Calvin's idea of the church as a disciplined community? Is the church of today too tolerant toward inconsistencies in Christian living?

What duties does a Christian today have to his community and to his nation? Was Calvin right that these duties are limited by a higher duty to God?

Can an earnest Christian worship God better through an elaborate ritual or through a simpler ritual such as Calvin preferred?

CHAPTER III

Did the organization of their church strengthen the Huguenots? Is the church as an organization necessary today?

In persecuting the Huguenots what did the French Government lose economically? morally? religiously? Did any permanent gain result from this policy of persecution?

Can you see any connection between the bloodthirsty persecutions of Huguenots and the atheism of the French Revolution which followed? Does our conduct as individual Christians today have any effect in drawing men to Christ or in repelling them from him?

Why, do you suppose, did businessmen incline to favor religious toleration? Did Holland gain by granting religious toleration? Did Holland's religious toleration help other countries? Was anything lost?

In the lands of Europe where Presbyterianism never did secure a permanent foothold, do you think the labors and sufferings of the early workers were wasted in God's sight? Explain.

CHAPTER IV

After reading about Knox's "call," how do you think God "calls" men today to the Christian ministry?

Is any government justified in trying to change a people's religion by force, as James I and Charles I sought to do in Scotland? What should a Christian do if a government tries to dictate his religious faith by force?

Do you think that any of the Christian denominations of America should be merged, following the example of the Scottish churches? Name some.

Why are the people of northern Ireland called "Scotch-Irish"? Do you think that the Catholics of Ulster were fairly treated?

Are there causes of tension between Protestants and Roman Catholics in America today? What can be done to promote good will?

CHAPTER V

Is it possible today to bring all Christians to believe alike and to worship alike, as Queen Elizabeth tried to do? Is it possible for Christians to practice mutual good will and co-operation while still retaining their various differences of belief and worship?

Has Christianity contributed to the rise of political democracy? Is democracy identical with Christianity?

From what country was English Presbyterianism replenished? Tell the story.

After reading of the founding of Presbyterianism in Wales, do you think that religious revivals can have permanent results?

Do you think the British dominions are likely to assume an increasingly important place in world history? If so, what is the potential importance of the flourishing Presbyterianism among them?

CHAPTER VI

What combination of events made it certain that England's American colonies would be Protestant?

What racial groups brought Presbyterianism to America?

Give reasons from early American church history why Presbyterianism today is numerically weak in New England and numerically strong in the Middle Atlantic States.

How did the creation of a presbytery help American Presbyterianism? What are some of the benefits of efficient administration of Christ's work today?

CHAPTER VII

Name some reasons for the growth of early American Presbyterianism.

Would more of the early Presbyterian seriousness and reverence benefit our church life today?

Will a true Christian necessarily be able to point to the date of his conversion, as some of the leaders of the Great Awakening taught? If not, what is the distinguishing characteristic of a Christian?

Is emotion harmful or beneficial to the Christian life? Illustrate your answer from the Great Awakening.

Which is easier in church work, division or co-operation? Which serves the Kingdom better?

Should the frontier missionaries be numbered among the heroes of Christian history? Give reasons.

CHAPTER VIII

What was the attitude of Presbyterians toward the cause of American independence?

Tell something of the contribution of the Presbyterian Church to religious toleration in America.

By 1788 the Presbyterian Church possessed five documents as standards. Name the five. Name the four church "courts," or "judicatories," of which the General Assembly is the highest.

Give your impressions of the revival of 1798-1801. What were some of its good effects?

What were the chief causes of the church's remarkable growth during the period covered by this chapter?

CHAPTER IX

What were the advantages of the Plan of Union of 1801? State the relation of a local church under the Plan to the Congregational and Presbyterian denominations respectively.

State some of the results accomplished by Mills and his "haystack meeting." Name some practical ways in which young people today can devote their lives to Christ.

Describe the conditions which confronted frontier missionaries. What does America of today owe them?

Name at least five examples of nondenominational co-operation in America in the early nineteenth century.

Can education, by itself, make a person a Christian? If a person is a Christian, can education make him a more useful Christian?

CHAPTER X

Name some of the changes that appeared in American public life after 1830; some parallel changes in church life.

Do you think that the Presbyterian Church gained anything by dividing in 1837? What did it lose?

What lands were added to the United States during this period? Did the churches meet the new responsibility? Explain.

What caused the revival of 1857? What can laymen do to bring about spiritual awakening today?

Tell the story of the separation of the Southern Church. What ties bind us closely to this sister denomination?

CHAPTER XI

Name some factors that helped to reunite "Old School" and "New School" Presbyterians. Are any of these forces operating to unite denominations today?

When a Christian's beliefs are challenged by new ideas, what should he do about it? In what ways might such a crisis strengthen his Christian faith? How might it deepen his spiritual life?

How can the church help business and labor to understand each other better? to work for the welfare of all?

What special problems has the growth of cities created for the church? what special opportunities?

List some things that your local church could do to improve the relations among the churches in your community.

Select from the Presbyterian *Book of Common Worship* a few prayers that appeal particularly to you, and read these thoughtfully and reverently at a worship service of your church group. Study and compare orders of worship on different church bulletins. What is to be said in favor of formal, read worship? in favor of a simpler, more spontaneous service? What is essential for any true Christian worship?

Describe briefly the work of each of the Boards of the church.

CHAPTER XII

What is the difference between belief about God and trust in God? Are both necessary for the Christian? Explain.

Name local forces that are making relations better between different denominations in your own community. Name forces that increase separation among them.

To Christianize peoples in other lands is it necessary to Americanize them? How can we help them to develop a Christianity of their own?

How can the church apply Christian principles to American business life without taking sides between "capital" and "labor" and other rival groups?

Are there ways in which Christian faith should limit patriotism? ways in which it should increase patriotism?

In your community is the church leading or lagging in racial desegregation? How do you explain this?

Can you see any connection between the emphasis of the Presbyterian and Reformed Churches on the Bible and their strong emphasis on education?

What do you consider to be the most important tasks confronting the Presbyterian Church in the immediate future?

CHAPTER XIII

In what ways did the "Covenanters" and "Seceders" show courage and Christian devotion in Scotland and in America? (See also Chapter IV.)

Did their strong convictions create any difficulties? What should be the attitude today of a Christian toward social customs that some people consider morally or spiritually dubious? By what tests should the Christian decide this question?

What are some of the problems faced by pioneer home missionaries and foreign missionaries? What are their rewards?

What does the history of the United Presbyterian Church teach about how to achieve Christian unity? What spirit is necessary? What should be sacrificed for larger Christian unity? What may not properly be sacrificed?

What was the importance of the merger of 1957 that created the United Presbyterian Church in the U.S.A.? What can you do that the new church may have greater influence for Jesus Christ?

CHAPTER XIV

Name four Presbyterian denominations that sprang from the Presbyterian Church in the United States of America.

Name four Presbyterian denominations of Scottish "Covenanter" or "Secession" origin. (See Chapter XIII.)

Name two Presbyterian denominations of Continental origin. Are these churches Americanized today? Give proof.

Is Presbyterianism a world-wide faith today? Give some detailed evidence.

Characterize Presbyterian church government, doctrine, and worship.

Bibliography

NOTE: In the foregoing study, the most recent statistics for the Presbyterian Church in the U. S. A. are taken from the *Minutes of the General Assembly* (1956). Unless otherwise indicated, statistics for other churches in the United States are from the *Yearbook of American Churches, Edition for 1958,* edited by B. Y. Landis, National Council of Churches of Christ in the U. S. A., 1957; statistics outside of the United States are from *Proceedings . . . of the Alliance of the Reformed Churches . . . 1954,* Geneva, Switzerland, Office of the Alliance, 1954.

BACKGROUND STUDIES

Bainton, Roland H., *The Church of Our Fathers*. The Westminster Press, 1950.

Bainton, Roland H., *Here I Stand: A Life of Martin Luther*. Abingdon Press, 1950.

Dowey, Edward A., Jr., *The Knowledge of God in Calvin's Theology*. Columbia University Press, 1952.

Kerr, Hugh T., Jr., *A Compend of the Institutes of the Christian Religion*. Presbyterian Board of Christian Education, 1939.

Kerr, Hugh T., Jr., *Positive Protestantism: An Interpretation of the Gospel*. The Westminster Press, 1950.

Latourette, Kenneth S., *A History of Christianity*. Harper & Brothers, 1953.

Nichols, James Hastings, *History of Christianity 1650–1950*. The Ronald Press Company, 1956.

Nichols, James Hastings, *Primer for Protestants*. Association Press, 1947.

Niesel, Wilhelm, *The Theology of Calvin*. Translated by Harold Knight. The Westminster Press, 1956.

Parker, T. H. L., *Portrait of Calvin*. The Westminster Press, 1955.

Schaff, Philip, *History of the Christian Church*. 8 vols. Charles Scribner's Sons, 1886–1924.

Sweet, William W., *The Story of Religion in America*. Harper & Brothers, 1950.

Walker, Williston, *A History of the Christian Church*. Charles Scribner's
    Sons, 1918.
Walker, Williston, *John Calvin*. G. P. Putnam's Sons, 1906.

WORLD-WIDE PRESBYTERIANISM

Alliance of the Reformed Churches Holding the Presbyterian Order
    (World Presbyterian Alliance), *Proceedings* of the successive Gen-
    eral Councils (includes statistics).
Dakin, Arthur, *Calvinism*. London, Gerald Duckworth and Company,
    Ltd., 1941. The Westminster Press, 1946.
Maxwell, William D., *An Outline of Christian Worship*. Oxford Uni-
    versity Press, 1936.
McNeill, John T., *The History and Character of Calvinism*. Oxford Uni-
    versity Press, 1954.
Moffatt, James, *The Presbyterian Churches*. London, Methuen & Co.,
    Ltd., 1928.
Ogilvie, J. N. *The Presbyterian Churches of Christendom*. Revised edition,
    London, A. and C. Black, 1925.
Reed, R. C., *History of the Presbyterian Churches of the World*. The
    Westminster Press, 1905.

PRESBYTERIAN CHURCH IN THE U. S. A.

Armstrong, M. W., Loetscher, L. A., and Anderson, C. A., eds., *The
    Presbyterian Enterprise: Sources of American Presbyterian History*.
    The Westminster Press, 1956.
Briggs, Charles A., *American Presbyterianism: Its Origin and Early His-
    tory*. Charles Scribner's Sons, 1885.
Drury, Clifford M., *Presbyterian Panorama: One Hundred and Fifty
    Years of National Missions History*. Board of Christian Education
    of the Presbyterian Church in the U. S. A., 1952.
Gillet, E. H., *History of the Presbyterian Church in the United States of
    America*. Revised ed., 2 vols. Presbyterian Board of Publication and
    Sabbath-School Work, 1864.
Hanzsche, William Thomson, *The Presbyterians: The Story of a Stanch
    and Sturdy People*. The Westminster Press, 1934.
Klett, Guy S., *Presbyterians in Colonial Pennsylvania*. University of Penn-
    sylvania Press, 1937.
Lake, Benjamin J., *The Story of the Presbyterian Church in the U. S. A*.
    The Westminster Press, 1956.
Loetscher, Frederick W., "Presbyterianism in America," in *An Outline of
    Christianity, the Story of Our Civilization*. Bethlehem Publishers,
    1926.
Loetscher, Frederick W., "The Period of the General Assembly, 1789–
    1931," in *Journal of the Department of History* (March, 1932).

Loetscher, Lefferts A., *The Broadening Church: A Study of Theological Issues in the Presbyterian Church Since 1869*. University of Pennsylvania Press, 1954.

Miller, Park Hays, *Why I Am a Presbyterian*. Thomas Nelson & Sons, 1956.

Presbyterian Church in the U. S. A., *Minutes of the General Assembly*, annual volumes. Office of the General Assembly.

    Constitution. Revised periodically. Board of Christian Education of the Presbyterian Church in the U. S. A.

    Presbyterian Law for the Local Church, ed. by Eugene C. Blake. Revised periodically. Board of Christian Education in the U. S. A.

Slosser, Gaius J., ed., *They Seek a Country: The American Presbyterians, Some Aspects*. The Macmillan Company, 1955.

Sweet, William W., *Religion on the American Frontier*. Vol. II. *The Presbyterians 1783–1840*. Harper & Brothers, 1936.

Thompson, Robert E., *A History of the Presbyterian Churches in the U. S.* Charles Scribner's Sons, 1895.

Trinterud, Leonard J., *The Forming of an American Tradition: A Re-examination of Colonial Presbyterianism*. The Westminster Press, 1949.

Webster, Richard, *A History of the Presbyterian Church in America, from Its Origin Until the Year 1760*. Joseph M. Wilson, 1857.

Zenos, Andrew C., *Presbyterianism in America: Past—Present and Prospective*. Thomas Nelson & Sons, 1937.

UNITED PRESBYTERIAN CHURCH OF NORTH AMERICA

Harper, R. D., *The Church Memorial*. Follett, Foster and Co., 1858.

McCulloch, W. E., *The United Presbyterian Church and Its Work in America*. United Presbyterian Board of Publication and Bible School Work, 1925.

McCulloch, W. E., "The United Presbyterian Church in America," in V. Ferm, ed., *The American Church of the Protestant Heritage*. Philosophical Library, 1953, pp. 209–222.

Scouller, James R., *History of the United Presbyterian Church of North America*. Charles Scribner's Sons, 1894.

Williamson, Clarence J., *March On with the United Presbyterian Church of North America*. United Presbyterian Board of Publication and Bible School Work, 1933.